Life principles for
living out
the
Greatest
commandment

D1571471

What Others Are Saying about *Following God: Life Principles for Living Out the Greatest Commandment:*

"Many books and study guides have been written about how to discover the road to a meaningful spiritual life. Occasionally something truly exceptional comes along. That is exactly what I discovered upon reading Cheri Strange's study. She has a heart for God; and it shows. Even though she speaks deliberately to women, the biblical truths taught are right on target and applicable whether the reader is male or female. Do you want to know how to love God more effectively? Do you want to be empowered by His presence in your life? Then make plans today to get a copy of this study and start reading and listening."

Randy A. Hughes, Ph.D., Minister and founder of
Shepherd's Rest Ministry, ShepherdsRM.org.

"It is a joy and privilege to serve as pastor to Dr. Cheri Strange and her family. Cheri is a godly co-laborer in the work of the Lord. I commend not only Cheri herself but I also commend *Life Principles for Living Out the Greatest Commandment.* As is always the case for Cheri Strange, Scripture is supreme in her teaching. Cheri is gifted by God to plumb the depths of the Bible and then to present it to everyone in a way that is easily understood and challenging to the heart. I am excited about what God can do through this study as women come face to face with the real meaning of what it means to love God with all of one's heart, soul, mind, and strength. May God bless every student of *Life Principles for Living Out the Greatest Commandment.*"

Andy Davis, Sr. Pastor, FBC Belton, Texas.

Life principles for
for
living out
the
Greatest
commandment

CHERI STRANGE

AMG
PUBLISHERS
ADVANCING THE MINISTRIES
OF THE GOSPEL

FOLLOWING GOD
Life Principles for Living Out the Greatest Commandment

© 2015 by Cheri Strange

Published by AMG Publishers. All Rights Reserved.
No part of this publication, including the artwork, may be reproduced, stored in a
retrieval system, or transmitted in any form or by any means, electronic, mechanical,
photocopying, recording, or otherwise—except for brief quotations in printed reviews,
without the prior written permission of the publisher.

ISBN: 978-0-89957-186-7
First Printing, June 2015

All Scripture quotations, unless otherwise indicated, are taken from the Holy Bible, New
International Version®, NIV®. Copyright ©1973, 1978, 1984, 2011 by Biblica, Inc.™
Used by permission of Zondervan. All rights reserved worldwide. www.zondervan.com
The "NIV" and "New International Version" are trademarks registered in the United
States Patent and Trademark Office by Biblica, Inc.™

Scriptures marked (MSG) are taken from THE MESSAGE.
Copyright © by Eugene H. Peterson,
1993, 1994, 1995. NavPress Publishing Group.

Scripture quotations marked (AMP) are taken from the Amplified Bible, Copyright ©
1954, 1958, 1962, 1964, 1965, 1987 by The Lockman Foundation. Used by permission.

Scripture quotations marked (KJV) are taken from the Holy Bible, King James Version,
which is in the public domain.

Cover design by Daryl Phillips, Chattanooga, TN

Editing by Diane Stortz and Rick Steele

Typesetting and page layout by Jennifer Ross

Printed in the United States of America
20 19 18 17 16 15 –WO– 6 5 4 3 2 1

CONTENTS

ACKNOWLEDGMENTS   vii

ABOUT THE AUTHOR   viii

INTRODUCTION   x

WEEK 1 • WHEN LIFE IS UNHINDERED   1

WEEK 2 • WHEN HEARTS WAVER   21

WEEK 3 • WHEN HEARTS HOLD NOTHING BACK   41

WEEK 4 • WHEN MINDS SHORT-CIRCUIT   61

WEEK 5 • WHEN THOUGHTS OVERCOME   83

WEEK 6 • WHEN STRENGTH MOVES MOUNTAINS   107

WEEK 7 • WHEN LOVE SATISFIES THE SOUL   131

WEEK 8 • WHEN LIFE OVERFLOWS   155

WORKS CITED   177

ACKNOWLEDGMENTS

Many thanks go to my good friends Wendi Fitzwater and Megan Teal, who endured the early vision and ghastly first drafts produced as I was just beginning to learn how to write. Their biblical grounding, strong editing skills, and encouragement helped me continue writing during those years, alone in my backyard with an audience of one.

I owe a special thanks to Andi Hale, my assistant with Beyond Ordinary Ministries. She has been my help in so many ways—from pouring over the details of the manuscript and helping with homework to playing hide-and-seek with the kids.

Much appreciation is due others also, including Dr. Randy Hughes, who read every page to ensure the contents were theologically sound and correctly represented the Bible. His encouragement, insight into Scripture, and understanding of how to connect with people were invaluable. Also, I am so thankful for the Bible Study Girls of First Baptist Church of Belton, Texas, who piloted the study, discussing every question at length, making the chapters more clear and the transitions smooth. For the keen eyes and expertise of Brannon Golden and Karen Porter, I am grateful. Karen, with her constant encouragement, helped me find my voice, while Brannon guided me to make the manuscript more clear and readable.

And to my friends at First Baptist Church, Belton, the Nearly-Newly class, the women who have prayed over me and allowed me to use them as examples for this study, and to my pastor, Andy Davis, thank you for all the prayers and support given me in the process of learning to do what God has called me to do.

I am extremely thankful for my mother-in-law, Fran Strange, and my parents, Bob and Carolyn Merrill, for helping make the sun stand still—by taking the children and doing the afternoon driving to give me a little more daylight for concentrated writing. To my sister, Kim Ross, who always encourages me and helps me in my weaknesses, thank you. And to my children: Taylor, Addison, Jolee, Sophia, Zoe, Chloe, Tate, and Zack, I owe many thanks. They selflessly encouraged me to be obedient, even when it required them to sacrifice, and they willingly helped keep everything together without me so I could finish the manuscript.

Finally, to my husband, Chad, who believed me when I thought I heard a whisper behind me saying, "This is the way. Walk in it," I am eternally grateful. He has been my cheerleader and the one on the front lines to help me find courage, not to stand still in terror but to keep walking—even when there were no doors open and every window shut. He has joyfully taken the responsibilities of running the house and caring for the children so I could have the time and concentration writing requires.

Not to us, LORD, not to us but to your name be the glory, because of your love and faithfulness (Psalm 115:1).

ABOUT THE AUTHOR

Dr. Cheri Strange earned her PhD from Baylor University in educational psychology. She received a MEd and a bachelor of behavioral arts from Hardin Simmons University. She has taught at Hardin Simmons University and Baylor University, as well as at the secondary and elementary levels of public school. A mother to two biological children (Taylor and Addison), and six adopted children (Jolee, Sophia, Zoe, Chloe, Tate, and Zack) ages six to fourteen, Cheri's days are filled with much activity, laughter, trips to Wal-Mart, and a healthy dose of organized chaos.

Cheri is a passionate presenter who communicates the Word of God powerfully and practically, speaking at women's conferences and various women's events. Dr. Strange is the Director of Women's Ministries at First Baptist Church in Belton, Texas, mentoring and equipping women to get to know their God and understand His will for their lives.

This study is Cheri's first Bible study, born out of years of wrestling with understanding at least some of the differences between loving God and loving God wholeheartedly. This is not a study written from the view of an ivory tower, peering down as an onlooker—but from her knees, looking up for truth, wisdom, and direction from the only one who can give it: the one who loves us first.

Dr. Strange operates Beyond Ordinary Ministries, encouraging women through her writing and speaking events to leave comfortable lives of Christian mediocrity and stretch beyond the ordinary Christian experience to live the life Jesus desires. She has been married for over twenty years. Cheri and her husband, Chad, live in Temple, Texas, with their eight children, his dogs, and her cats. You can find more information and resources available from Dr. Strange at CheriStrange.com.

INTRODUCTION

Life Principles for Living out the Greatest Commandment: That's a mouthful—enough to cause a twinge of discomfort, even in the most committed of Christ followers. *Don't be afraid to read further.* Chances are, you are very much like me, and I *need* what's written in these pages. In fact, I need these principles blown up **poster-sized** as reminders of what my life is to be about.

Some of what I need is similar to needing a root canal. I don't want to do it, but when I'm in pain, the only solution is to poke around, dig out the garbage, saw the remnants away, and replace the bad and ineffective tooth with a golden crown.

But I am also in desperate need of something spiritually similar to a long day at a spa, complete with all the soothing massages and rejuvenating treatments. *Keep reading*, because this book offers some combination of both.

This study is for the one who wants to know how to love God completely. It's for the one who wants to *want* to know how to love Him. It's for the one who considers herself clueless in terms of knowing where to begin living out the Greatest Commandment. At the same time, it's perfect for the one who *thinks* she knows but wants to be sure she doesn't miss anything.

Honestly, the principles found within these pages will likely meet you where you are. They are written to the mistake-ridden, the failures, and the disappointed—who are straining for hope. They are for the discontented—tired of pretending they have it all together; and for the one who's disheartened by a life that is *not* as purpose filled or fruitful as she would like. The following pages are for anyone longing to learn how to love deeply while, at the same time, waiting to be saturated in His presence, covered by His goodness, and lavished with His love.

This is why you're here. He has been drawing you to this very place. Your God knows you, your deepest deficits as well as your most desperate needs, and loves you completely. He knows you should be beyond this point in your life but meets you right where you sit today. *Get ready to turn the page.* He is more than ready to use these principles to help us make spiritual progress, growing us to more fully possess His amazing love, and teaching us how to respond to it.

Soli Deo Gloria,

LESSON 1

WHEN LIFE IS UNHINDERED

Welcome, my friend. You are probably here for the same reasons I am. You want to become the woman God envisions you to be, but you're not quite there. Most days, you and I are not anywhere close. You would love godliness to waft into you through your pillow by osmosis while you sleep at night, but it hasn't happened yet. You're still just the broken-down version of you, and I'm still the broken-down version of me.

Neither of us has likely greeted a day loving God with everything we are, but today you and I have decided to learn. We want to love Him completely. So we begin this journey together, to learn how to live out the Greatest Commandment. Before we get started, there is something you need to know.

The King has been waiting for you. He wants you to know you are His treasured possession. He has seen you in your pajamas and ponytail. He knows that all these years later you are still carrying the "baby weight" you gained. He's seen your gray hairs and how feverishly you try to camouflage the dark circles under your eyes. It doesn't matter. The King has chosen you. Your Savior is crazy about you. He loves you before you can love Him back, every time.

He loves you just as you are, not as you wish you were.

He loves you in the middle of your broken promises.

He loves you in the midst of your brokenheartedness.

He loves you when the one who promised to does not.

He loves you even when you do not love Him back.

He loves you completely. He has been waiting for you expectantly. Before you pick up a pen and fill in any blanks, you need to know He totally digs you. He loves your personality, your eyes, your body mass index, your irritating habits no one else seems to appreciate, your unique style, that quirky humor, and your signature laugh.

The King loves you and has come for you today:

> *Listen, daughter, and pay careful attention: Forget your people and your father's house. Let the king be enthralled by your beauty; honor him, for he is your lord.*
>
> Psalm 45:10–11

Over the next eight weeks, He asks that you show up right here. Wherever "here" is for you, the King will be there to meet with you. Learning to live out the Greatest Commandment sounds like a lot of work on our part. Actually, it is about a love completely driven from the relationship initiator, for we can only love Him because He started it. He loved us first.

DAY 1

LOVE BRINGS HOPE

We love because he first loved us. 1 John 4:19

The apostle John tells us that not only does the God of the universe love us before we love Him, love is who He is (1 John 4:16). Love is not simply a quality of God's character. John could have described God as loving, just as He claims himself to be compassionate and slow to anger (Exodus 34:6). He could have noted that God loves as an optional choice. The difference is more than semantics. Love is not what God *does*. Love is His *very nature*. It is His essence. Where He can act compassionately or choose to be merciful, God, who *is* love, takes care not to separate love from what He says or how He acts. Perhaps this reality of who God is explains why love is what He most desires from us. Is this perhaps why He asks us to love Him with everything *we* are—because love is everything *He* is?

We begin our study together in Deuteronomy 6:4–5. Please write these verses below.

Like many of you, I have read past these verses many times. I know loving God is supposed to be the most important priority of my life. The instruction to love God with all my heart, soul, mind, and strength has been drilled into me since I was a preacher's kid (literally living on the church property). But this seemingly straightforward admonition always seemed too hard and out of reach for someone like me. That kind of relationship was for someone else—like Billy Graham, selfless missionaries, or gifted pastors. Surely it would be enough for me to demonstrate my love by being a good Christian girl, trying to do all the right things a preacher's kid should do, and having a spotty relationship with Him like most other regular people. What more could He expect from someone like *me*?

When I married, the reality of someone observing firsthand whether I actually lived what I claimed to believe splashed over me like a bucket of icy water. I needed help being consistent with my time alone with God so that my husband would know he married a good Christian girl; so I purchased a One Year® Bible. After nine years of failure, I could finally keep pace with the reading schedule. But in those nine years of trying to keep up appearances, I discovered that my view of God, myself, and what God dreamed for me was too small. Much. Too. Small.

Tucked inside the history of Israel's kings live two short verses this good Christian girl had skimmed across all her life. These words would ultimately turn my thinking about myself and about my God upside down:

> *Amaziah . . . reigned in Jerusalem twenty-nine years. . . . He did what was right in the eyes of the LORD, but not wholeheartedly.*
>
> 2 Chronicles 25:1–2

Did you catch that? Amaziah "did what was right in the eyes of the Lord, **but not wholeheartedly.**" That summary of his life presented a close reflection of my own. Panic set in, because I was a self-declared good Christian girl! I was not engaged in any heinous sin. I loved Jesus, but I knew I did not love Him with *all* of anything. My alarm grew when words of Jesus began to penetrate my heart:

> *One of the teachers of the law . . . asked him, "Of all the commandments, which is the most important?"*
>
> *"The most important one," answered Jesus, "is this: 'Hear, O Israel: The Lord our God, the Lord is one. Love the Lord your God with all your heart and with all your soul and with all your mind and with all your strength.'"*
>
> Mark 12:28–30

According to Jesus, this is the big one of the top ten rules. *NOT* loving Him with *all* is breaking a commandment. *Not* loving Him wholeheartedly is a sin. Somehow I had categorized His words as a suggestion for the supergodly. Lacking that level of godliness left me off the hook, safe in my tiny world of halfhearted mediocrity. Of course, I was wrong. Offering God anything less than my all is equivalent to murder, adultery, stealing, and idolatry.

Do you find that reality as unnerving as I did? I thought wholehearted pursuit was *optional*. Suddenly confronted with the truth, I did not know what to do, but I began to ask Him. Really, I begged Him, "Lord, show me the difference between loving You with everything I am and settling for halfhearted mediocrity."

What you have in these pages is my attempt to pass along what this halfhearted, small-thinking, Jesus girl is learning. Read Deuteronomy 4:29 and 2 Chronicles 16:9. These two verses set in motion my own journey toward wholehearted pursuit. How do they encourage you?

_____

_____

_____

I know what you are thinking: loving God with all your heart, soul, mind, and strength sounds hard, maybe even impossible. Stay with me, because the Israelites felt the same way when God said it the first time. Moses encouraged the Israelites in three ways, each of which you and I can still benefit from today.

GOD DRAWS US TO HIMSELF AND ENABLES US TO LOVE HIM WITH ALL

God always makes the first move. In Genesis, He initiates an indissoluble covenant relationship with Abraham, and later He extends it to the Israelites as they are about to enter the Promised Land. Read Genesis 17:4–8 and Deuteronomy 29:12–14. List the words in these verses that point to the initiator of the covenant.

_____

_____

_____

_____

Make no mistake about it. Those "who are not here today" means you and me. God is still in the covenant-initiating business. He continues to make the first move, love us, take us as His own, and promise to be our God.

Read Deuteronomy 30:6. What does God promise in this verse?

_____

_____

_____

God pointed the Israelites toward the possibility for faith that He was orchestrating. One commentator wrote, "He will prepare their hearts to believe and remove the barriers to full commitment and faith. With this liberating work of God the returning generation will be able to carry out the full requirements of the pleadings of Deuteronomy."[1]

Incredible! Can you comprehend that not only does God initiate a relationship with you personally, He also takes away your evil, unbelieving heart and replaces it with a believing one? With this new, renovated heart, you are equipped for experiencing the joy of loving Him with all your heart, soul, mind, and strength!

LOVING HIM WITH OUR ALL IS WITHIN REACH

God provides the means. In Deuteronomy 30:11–12, 14 Moses encourages the people to recognize an important truth:

> Now what I am commanding you today is not too difficult for you or beyond your reach. It is not up in heaven, so that you have to ask, "Who will ascend into heaven to get it?". . . No, the word is very near you; it is in your mouth and in your heart so you may obey it.

Loving God with your all does not require a seminary degree, a dynamic leader, or a powerful worship experience. It's not as hard as we make it seem. After we have been equipped with new hearts capable of the kind of relationship God most desires, the secret we need to wholehearted loving is found in the Word of God. But simple reading will not be enough. To get the Word inside us will require thinking about it, talking about it, understanding what it requires and promises, and then acting on it. This is where the rubber meets the road in my life. This is where I had to stop making excuses for my satisfaction with mediocrity. Loving God with all heart, soul, mind, and strength is for _me_ and it is for _you_, not just for the superspiritual! Yes, God is the initiator and the enabler. But if I want anything greater than some meager epitaph summarizing my halfhearted life effort, I need to cooperate.

What about you? Is there one step you can take toward loving Him more today? What will you do?

_____

_____

_____

LOVING GOD WITH OUR ALL BRINGS THE PROMISE OF LIFE

God promises life and love. Read Deuteronomy 30:19–20. What did Moses encourage the Israelites to choose?

_____

_____

Today let me encourage you with one more word from Jesus:

> *I came that they may have and enjoy life, and have it in abundance (to the full, till it overflows).*
>
> John 10:10, AMP

What if there were a connection between the love-initiating and love-enabling Father and the life-giving Son? Maybe, just maybe, loving Him with all your heart, all your soul, all your mind, and all your strength is the catalyst necessary for experiencing the life God dreams for you. Today, allow the one who is love to bring the hope that gives you life—filled-to-the-tip-top-and-spilling-out-onto-the-floor life.

Spend your closing moments in a prayer of expectation for what the God who is love will bring on this journey.

_____

_____

_____

_____

_____

_____

_____

_____

DAY 2

SIN IS SERIOUS

If God draws us to a relationship that loves Him wholeheartedly and supplies what we need to do it, then why don't we do it? What keeps us content in our tiny puddles of mediocrity convinced that living life to the full and the business of loving God wholeheartedly is for the few?

For many of us, our largest hindrance is sin. It could involve an unhealthy relationship, a critical spirit (with a mouth to match), destructive and addictive habits, or something more serious. Maybe it's simply how we choose to react to a situation that drives us to sin. Of course, all of us fall into sin from time to time. First John 1:8 says it plainly: "If we claim to be without sin, we deceive ourselves and the truth is not in us."

Sometimes we do more than fall into sin—we run to it with reckless abandon. Other times we find ourselves engulfed by it, uncertain how it happened.

Committing the sinful act is only part of what makes sin our greatest hindrance to loving God completely. What we do *with* our sin and what we do *as a result* of it can also contribute to lives that settle for less than we should. If we want to protect ourselves from halfhearted pursuit and small aspirations for the kingdom, what must we do, according to 1 John 1:9?

_____

_____

_____

_____

This promise is all encompassing and without limitations. There is no way we can fail one too many times or surpass His willingness to wipe away our ugliness. If we confess our sin, regardless of what it is, God will forgive us. If you confess yours, you can rest assured. You will be forgiven.

While asking forgiveness and confessing our failings is the first step toward getting on with loving God completely, when I find myself swimming in the results of my own bad behavior, I shrink away from intimacy with God and revert back to wallflower mode. Oh, I may continue through the motions, but my heart will remain at a distance. It was through my daughter Jolee that I first recognized my hindering behavior.

Jolee was not adopted out of the orphanage until she was nine. She remembers what it was like to be an orphan: unloved, unwanted, insignificant. I began noticing that each time she was corrected, her body language and solitude practically screamed that she did not feel part of our family. Afterward, it might take days to draw her back. Watching her illuminated my own habits of detachment when I make mistakes before God. When I pull away from God each time I fail, I compound the problem of my sin by living like He could not love me or use me.

Psalm 51:1–13 helps us learn how to move forward unhindered after we sin. What can David's example teach us?

_____

_____

_____

Scripture teaches that everyone is born with a sin nature and in need of a Savior (Psalm 51:5). Paul points us to Christ in Romans 7:24–25:

> *What a wretched man I am! Who will rescue me from this body*
> *that is subject to death? Thanks be to God, who delivers me*
> *through Jesus Christ our Lord!*

Many Christians do not realize they have been liberated from the "body that is subject to death," their predisposition to sin. They stay in their pit of sin (Psalm 103:4) and live a sad existence as "saved sinners," doomed. Although we are born with a completely fallen nature, Jesus came to set us free. Peter also assures us:

> *His divine power has given us everything we need for a godly*
> *life through our knowledge of him who called us by his own*
> *glory and goodness.*

> 2 Peter 1:3

So what's the deal with sin and the life of a Christian? Read Genesis 4:1–7. The first two sons, Cain and Abel, gave something back to God, but there is a marked difference between the givers and between the gifts. One gave his best out of a heart that loved God completely. The other gave less than his best out of a heart that loved God in part.

Genesis 4:7 gives us three elements of sin. Please list them.

1. Sin _____ at your door.

2. It _____ to have you.

3. _____ it.

The Hebrew word for *crouching* means "to cause to rest or lie down." It suggests sin is lying in wait for you, right on your threshold. Sin is not going somewhere else; it is waiting for you. My friend, sin longs for you. These verses teach that we must master it. Wait—*what?* Is that possible? Can we master sin?

Read Genesis 4:6–7 again. God says Cain can overcome what is lying in wait for him. Each of us has sinned in some way at some point (Romans 3:23). Yet the Word implores us to leave sin:

> And Jesus said unto her, "Neither do I condemn thee:
> go, and sin no more."
>
> John 8:11, KJV

> My dear children, I write this to you so that you will not sin.
>
> 1 John 2:1

I agree with Billy Graham: "God never would have told us to reject evil acts if in point of fact we could not help but do them. Thank God we need not sin, even though we can sin."[2] Believers remain *capable* of sin but not *doomed* to it. In fact, Scripture is clear that we can exercise control over sin in our lives:

> No temptation has overtaken you except what is common to
> mankind. And God is faithful; he will not let you be tempted
> beyond what you can bear. But when you are tempted, he will
> also provide a way out so that you can endure it.
>
> 1 Corinthians 10:13

We can test God in this. He is faithful to provide a way out of making sinful choices, because He wants us to be victorious. God never cheers for our failure. He promises to invariably, without exception, on all occasions, provide a way out of sin. But we must take it. Write what Romans 6:17–18 teaches about sin and the follower of Christ.

_____

_____

_____

What if I take God's Word seriously about sin and His ability to get me around it without succumbing to it? In some ways, this possibility is terrifying. Taking God seriously requires spiritual battle. Yet what if I didn't have to lose against sin every time? What if I took the option to fight back or walk away rather than simply get my spiritual teeth kicked in? We're not talking about perfection, by any means, but a realization that God's Word provides the channel to receive strength to navigate around temptation. We don't have to lose because God has already given us instructions for victory. We have the upper hand against Satan—God's hand.

Temptation is an area I battle daily. Satan does not want us to stand blameless before our merciful Father. The enemy whispers thoughts like these:

"That thing you did? It's not a big deal."

"Everybody says things like that."

"Everyone watches those kinds of programs."

"Other Christians think those thoughts."

"It's OK to get really frustrated with your children. There is no need to talk about it. Continue in your walk with God."

We seem to put sins on a continuum. God does not. What happens if the enemy convinces us to brush over these "small and insignificant" sins? No matter how vicious or slight our sin seems, *any* sin separates us from God. Although I *know* this truth, victory over sin is not a *reality* in my life unless I do two things:

   1. Recognize the lie being set up by Satan.

   2. Place my sinfulness before the Lord.

We should ask God to draw anything out we may not even recognize as sin. Then we wait. In the beginning, I had a laundry basket full of habitual junk I had glossed over. Today I rest in the truth that He faithfully makes me clean because of His deep love for me and His desire to be in close relationship with me.

Once we recognize that we can participate in winning battles against sin, we will see more victory—not perfection, but **more** victorious living on this side of heaven. Once more cognizant of our sinfulness and committed to the Lord to come clean, we will experience defeat by sin less and less. If we will believe God's promise to give us a way out of temptation every time, we might walk away from that hateful comment without retaliating. We might refuse to believe we are completely bound to failure.

Unfortunately, I am familiar with feeling like I just had the spiritual wind knocked out of me. To express myself to the Lord, I wrote the following words in my journal. You may want to pray a similar prayer too.

> *I've done it again, Lord. Again I chose NOT to believe you—and accepted Satan's view over yours. Help me catch a glimpse of how I can be free. Help me take the victory you so graciously give me every time so that I can choose YOU over sin! YOU are my worthy pursuit.*

Day 3

Belief Is Necessary

The most crippling factor in my Christian life is the failure to believe God and trust Him. So I have come to rely on Hebrews 11 as a powerful reminder of those who could have been hindered in their pursuit but instead chose to believe in what they could not see:

> *Now faith is the assurance (the confirmation, the tile deed) of the things [we] hope for, being the proof of things [we] do not see and the conviction of their reality [faith perceiving as real fact what is not revealed to the senses].*

Hebrews 11:1, AMP

Faith is what we choose to embrace as a real fact, even though everything we see gives evidence to the contrary. We hold to it so greatly that it influences who we are and what we do.

Take time today to read all of Hebrews 11. God provides more examples there than I can count on my fingers and toes of people of varying age, ability, talent, resources, and depravity who allowed faith to transform their lives. Hebrews testifies that there is an alignment between our hearts' decision to believe and the actions taken by our feet.

This juncture of heart and feet alignment is where my failure to believe lies. Once again, our daughter Jolee has taught me about myself and my God. After years in an orphanage environment, Jolee had no expectations of herself. Many things you and I might think a girl her age could do, she would refuse to try. When I urged to attempt something new, I brought her to tears. It was not my intention to bring her difficulties and struggles; I simply could see the bigger picture. Like every other child, there were certain things she needed to learn to do. On occasions when I felt confident she understood the task and was equipped to manage, I embraced her and said, "Mommy loves you. But you can do this!" I knew she should at least take a stab at the task. And with encouragement to live in expectation that she *could* and *would* succeed, she has.

We do the same thing with God. We should be ready and mature enough to do certain tasks God places before us, but we are afraid to try. Wouldn't we rather God step in and do them for us? Aren't we tempted to believe that if He doesn't, it's because we are unloved? Instead we perceive the expectation is simply too high, and we find ourselves in tears.

After watching my daughter, I see how often I have faltered in this area of belief. At times, I don't even want to try. "If He loved me, He would do this for me" reverberates in my head. But He knows the bigger picture. He is my Dad. In the course of spiritual maturity, there are certain things for which I need to believe Him, trusting I am His treasured possession (Malachi 3:17), even when He requires me to stretch beyond my comfort zone.

What about you? Has there been a time when you wanted God to just do a task for you, so that you did not have to believe Him? If so, describe it here.

_____

_____

_____

_____

What happens when we allow our faith to leave its fingerprint on our lives? Scripture is replete with examples, including the story of Joshua and the Israelites. The Israelites had crossed the Jordan and conquered Jericho and Ai when their judgment was tested by the Gibeonites. The leaders of Gibeon, a neighboring city, approached the Israelite camp pretending to be from a far-off nation. Without consulting with God, the Israelites forged a peace agreement with Gibeon. Shortly after this, the Israelites learned the truth. However, when the Gibeonites were attacked and called upon the Israelites for help, true to their agreement, the Israelites went to their defense (Joshua 10). The mistake of making a treaty with the Gibeonites *on their own, without* inquiring of the Lord, risked lives now and assured future repercussions.

Read Joshua 10:7-8. Notice how God dealt with the leader who really blew it through his disobedience and jeopardized the safety of the entire Israelite community. Did God remove Joshua from his command? Did He publically reprimand him, drawing attention to his mistakes? No.

He reassured Joshua he would have victory, encouraging him not to be afraid. I find that when I get myself into a mess, God doesn't waste time lecturing me about how I should have done better. He simply comes to my aid.

Suddenly Joshua and the Israelites had a choice to make. They could believe what God told Joshua and head confidently into battle, or they could refuse to believe God and embrace defeat. Joshua chose to believe God and put his feet into action:

> *After an all-night march from Gilgal,*
> *Joshua took them by surprise.*
>
> Joshua 10:9

Read what happened next (Joshua 10:10–14). Why do you believe Joshua asked God to make the sun stand still?

_____

_____

_____

Ponder this preposterous solution! Joshua was a military commander. He marched with his army for over twenty-four hours. If we were to plot the route to the battlefront on a map, it was uphill both ways. His men had gone without food and rest. However, Joshua believed (v. 8) God would deliver the enemies into Israel's hands. So why did he ask for something as outrageous as the sun to stand still, especially since he knew Israel was destined to win?

Recall Joshua's history with the Lord, serving as Moses' aide. When Moses died, God appointed Joshua the leader of the people. He had spent much of his time observing Moses' faith develop. To help us understand Joshua, glance back to Exodus 17:8–15, where we find a different battle ensuing.

While Joshua was fighting that battle, Moses, Aaron, and Hur were invoking God's power. When Moses' arms were up, the Israelites prevailed, but if his arms faltered and drooped, Israel began to lose. What did God tell Moses to do (v. 14)?

_____

_____

God wanted Joshua to know there are instances when although we have hearts full of faith and feet taking action, the victory comes only when we have faith to ask God to move as only He can. Joshua possessed faith that led to victory against the five kings in Joshua 10 because Moses possessed faith that led to victory over the Amalekites in Exodus 17.

How could a military commander have the courage to *request* the sun to stand still? Because he had experienced victory in battle due to something absurd: an old man holding his arms up in the air. In essence, Joshua said, "I hear you. You said we will be victorious. I am putting my belief into practice. We're giving all we've got, but Lord, we're about to lose the daylight—and we're not done yet. Could you help me out a little here? If you would keep that sun right there, we can do what you've called and equipped us to do, and we will be victorious."

When was the last time you witnessed a situation as impossible as the sun standing still to allow someone to complete what God required? Think about your own life situations. Are you taking

God at His Word in the face of the impossible? There is biblical precedent for requesting something as ludicrous as more daylight. There is biblical precedent for requesting the outlandish or absurd. I strongly encourage it!

Not every victory requires a sun-stopping miracle. Sometimes the all-night march will do. Sometimes not even a step is required, but what about the times when action is necessary? Do you have the faith and courage to believe God will bring victory? Whatever victory looks like in your situation, will you ask Him to do something awesome or preposterous for you?

_____

_____

_____

_____

_____

_____

He is believable and trustworthy. Yes, even for the outlandish.

DAY 4

FORGETTING IS REFUSED

Satan uses myriad tactics to distract us from pursuing God, but seldom is he very original. He employs the same strategies time and time again. Why? Put simply, because they work. When we discover some of his techniques and how to guard against them, we position ourselves to lead more believing, fruitful lives.

We find the strategy I want to focus on today in Exodus 14. The Israelites, a force of over two million people, plundered the Egyptians before leaving the country. When Pharaoh realized his entire workforce was gone, he roused his army, intending to pursue Israel and drag them back into slavery. Read Exodus 14:5–15, paying particular attention to how quickly the Israelites' attitudes eroded following their escape.

How did the Israelites march out of Egypt (v. 8)?

_____

What was the response of the Israelites when they saw Pharaoh (v. 10)?

_____

_____

What was their complaint to Moses about their situation (vv. 11–12)?

_____

_____

Within days of marching out of Egypt boldly, demonstrating confidence in a God who is true to His promises, the Israelites forgot His faithfulness and ability to deliver and descended into hopelessness and despair. Through circumstances and fearful indicators of what might occur, the Israelites succumbed to one of Satan's most paralyzing tactics: forgetfulness. They quickly forgot the fulfilled promises, miraculous signs, and guidance they had already received.

Unfortunately, I can relate to the tactic of forgetfulness. It is ridiculous how difficult it is to recall what God has promised when I listen to lies and stare at my current surroundings. Not only do I forget His faithfulness, but how many times must I be confronted with the same truths from Scripture without a personal impact? How many times must I read who I am in Christ before I live out those realties? How many days do I simply *not* grasp it . . . AGAIN? More than I would like to admit, on all counts.

NEVER FORGET

So what can we do? One way I've learned to defend myself against Satan's forgetfulness tactic is simply this: ***refuse to forget***. Read Deuteronomy 4:9. What we are not to forget?

_____

_____

What we are to do with this knowledge?

_____

_____

_____

We are also called to refuse to forget who God is and who we *were* and *are* because of Him. In Psalm 103, David refuses to forget. In the passages that follow, circle what God has done for us. Underline words that describe God's character.

> Praise the LORD, my soul, and forget not all his benefits—who forgives all your sins and heals all your diseases, who redeems your life from the pit and crowns you with love and compassion, who satisfies your desires with good things so that your youth is renewed like the eagle's.
>
> Psalm 103:2–5

> The LORD is compassionate and gracious, slow to anger, abounding in love. He will not always accuse, nor will he harbor his anger forever; he does not treat us as our sins deserve or repay us according to our iniquities. For as high as the heavens are above the earth, so great is his love for those who fear him; as far as the east is from the west, so far has he removed our transgressions from us.
>
> Psalm 103:8–12

The Israelites were told to refuse to forget, but they failed. How can we guard ourselves against forgetting? First, we should investigate Scripture. Participating in this Bible study is a prime example of how we practice refusing to forget. We distinguish between those things worth pursuing and those that are not. Then we lock that practice into our minds. Even more essential, we ask the Holy Spirit to help us remember who God is and who we are.

One practical thing I did was to ask God to keep fresh in my mind the pit from which He had pulled me. Remember, I was a self-proclaimed good girl. As I asked God to show me my sinfulness, I was horrified. The process was painful, but necessary. God reminded me of huge mistakes I had made that were wrong or hurtful to others. My sin became very real. However, my tendency was to place each sin on a sin continuum, so I mistakenly believed I was in pretty good shape. I felt I hadn't done anything *really bad*.

One weekend, the Lord nudged me in my spirit: "Cheri, if you want to know my **purpose** for you, you need to get in a **posture** before me that demonstrates you understand the **pit** from which I pulled you." Today I meet Him on my knees each morning, with few exceptions. He helps me remember the depths of my sin so that I continue to recognize my need for a Savior. I need saving. To keep myself from forgetting, I bow before Him. I thank Him for renewing me and transforming me into His likeness rather than leaving me as a pit dweller. Allow me to recommend remembering. I testify I am far from having life all together, but since I have committed to remembering, I have never been the same.

KEEP RECORDS OF HIS WORDS

Anytime you feel God is speaking a specific word to you, write it down. Underline verses in your Bible, and write in a journal. Write on note cards, or make sticky notes for your bathroom mirror, like my sister-in-law, Leslie, does. Plaster God's Word to the walls—whatever works for you. Get God's Word in a place where you can review it when you need it, because YOU NEED IT. Satan is against this strategy. He wants you to think God's Word is unnecessary.

God is emphatic about this business of refusing to forget. In Numbers 15:38–40 He tells the Israelites to make tassels for the corners of their garments, with a blue cord on each tassel. When they were faced with temptation to follow other gods, their clothing would remind them to obey God and only Him. Deuteronomy 6:6–9 offers other suggestions to encourage us to remember. List each one you identify.

_____

_____

_____

Finally, Isaiah 46:8–11 makes it very clear that choosing to remember is the personal responsibility of very believer and that God is worth the effort.

What do these verses suggest?

_____

_____

_____

We must work at not forgetting. I have a good memory, but I cannot keep straight whether I have clothes at the cleaners or not if I don't have a note. Without assistance, I will not be able to call up a particular Scripture if I don't do something to make myself learn it. I need to see the words over and over again. Because Satan is always working to thwart our belief in God, we need to find ways to remind ourselves of what God has said to us in order to move on victoriously. Refusing to forget God's Word is an active pursuit.

PLACE YOUR TRUST IN HIM

Trust is also an active pursuit. If we allow ourselves to forget who God is, who we are, what He has done, and what He has promised, we will falter in what He has called us to do. In Exodus 23:20–23, notice God's promises to the Israelites who had left Egypt. List all God had promised.

A. The angel (v. 20) will _____ and bring you _____ .

B. Pay attention (v. 21) and _____ to what He says.

C. If you listen and obey (v. 22), my angel will go ahead of you and _____ you into the land I have promised (v. 23).

Of course, we know that generation was not allowed to enter the land because they refused to believe God. In Numbers 13:33, the eight spies reported:

> *We saw the Nephilim there. . . . We seemed like grasshoppers in*
> *our own eyes, and we looked the same to them.*

Blinded by their fear and trepidation of the enemy, they rejected God's promises and refused to remember His faithfulness against impossible odds. Has there ever been a time in your life when you believe God declared something to you, but as you got into it, things looked bleak if not impossible? If so, describe what happened. What was the outcome?

_____

_____

_____

Although God continued to show himself mighty and able, the Israelites rejected Him and His promise to give them the land. What they saw around them was too great. They seemed like grasshoppers compared to what they were up against. Therefore, they died in the desert. I don't want to die in the desert because I forgot the glory, the miraculous signs, and the promises of God! God said to Moses, in his moment of doubt:

> *Is the LORD's arm too short? Now you will see whether or not*
> *what I say will come true for you.*

Numbers 11:23

The Lord's arm is not too short. No matter what you fear, His arm reaches down to surround your life and hold your circumstances. If your situation looks bleak, the time to remind yourself continually of that Word and His ability to fulfill it is now. Write it down, meditate on it, and keep it before you. You may want to start with the verse just mentioned, about God's arm. Then trust His arm will be just the right length needed to cause that Word to become a reality in your life. You may seem like a grasshopper. You may even *be* a grasshopper, but being a grasshopper has no influence on God's ability to perform His will. Choose **not to forget** the strength of your God.

Taking steps toward helping yourself NOT forget will allow God to be glorious through your life. What steps do you need to take toward refusing to forget today?

1. _____

2. _____

3. _____

Day 5

Fear Is Released

I get anxious at the thought of going through any invasive medical procedure, like getting my teeth cleaned. I have a history of swooning if not fainting outright on the table at most doctor appointments. After anticipating the appointment and arriving, I become nauseated by the sterile smell, and the experience deteriorates from there. You could say I battle a stronghold of fear in this area.

Honestly, most of my life I have battled fear in other areas as well. Had I given in to my greatest fears, I never would have married. I would have quit teaching after my miserable first year. I never would have applied for graduate school, and I likely would have remained childless. I am living proof of the reality of hindering fear and the ability to move beyond it. If we are ever going to be who God has called us to be and do what He has called us to do, we must be released from fear.

There is plenty to fear in our lives. Few need psychological attention to deal with unrealistic or imagined fears; most of us deal with genuinely scary issues. We don't know what to do about the fear, and we want to be free. What causes you to be fearful?

_____

_____

_____

Remember Joshua's strategic error made by signing a peace treaty with the Gibeonites without inquiring of the Lord? The Israelites found themselves defending these people against the five kings of the Amorites. We know how this story ends. After the army's all-night uphill march, God intervened miraculously. Reread Joshua 10:5–8, paying close attention to God's directive to Joshua in this dire situation:

> The LORD said to Joshua, "Do not be afraid of them;
> I have given them into your hand. Not one of them will be able
> to withstand you."
>
> Joshua 10:8

The Israelites were up against ominous circumstances. These were not molehills turned into mountains. These were not small enemies. They were ruthless and murderous bad guys. There was genuine reason to be scared to death. The enemies facing the Israelites generated a legitimate response: genuine fear.

We know Joshua *was* afraid, because God told him *not* to be. We also know Joshua overcame his fear to accomplish what God sent him to do. And he was not alone. We can be encouraged by the testimonies in Scripture of people who had legitimate reasons to be afraid yet chose not to let fear paralyze them. In the midst of fear and sometimes hair-raising situations, these heroes chose to release their fears to grasp the strong hand of the Lord, and their lives were forever different.

When we recognize that some of the greatest servants of God were afraid (sometimes over and over again), our own fear record may not seem so irrational and pathetic. Let's look at some of the fraidy cats of the Bible. In the list that follows, record who was afraid and what they feared. I have completed a few for you.

	Who Was Afraid?	Afraid of What?
Genesis 15:1	Abram	not having an heir
Genesis 32:11		
Exodus 2:14	Moses	Pharaoh
Judges 7:9–10		
1 Kings 19:2–3	Elijah	Jezebel
2 Chronicles 20:15	King Jehoshaphat	
Matthew 1:20		
Matthew 8:23–26		
Luke 1:30	Mary	the angel

Please note the common phrase found across these verses regarding what these people were called to do about their fear.

Do _____ ____ _____!

Note the number of times Ezekiel was instructed not to be afraid in his initial calling by God:

> And you, son of man, do not be afraid of them or their words.
> Do not be afraid, though briers and thorns are all around you
> and you live among scorpions. Do not be afraid of what they
> say or be terrified by them, though they are a rebellious house.
> You must speak my words to them, whether they listen or fail to
> listen, for they are rebellious.
>
> Ezekiel 2:6–7

We are told time and again not to fear. We **ARE NOT** told there is nothing to fear! How we respond to the fearful situations placed providentially in our paths is of paramount importance. In Acts 18, Paul recounts one such fearful situation. He has arrived in Corinth, earning his living making tents and speaking to Jews and Greeks there to believe the gospel message of Jesus. In time, the Jews forcefully oppose him, and he leaves the synagogue for a final time. Read Acts 18:7–11 to see how this drama unfolds.

Why was Paul not to be afraid?

_____

_____

What was at stake if he allowed fear to keep him from obedience?

_____

_____

The Bible gives evidence that some people choose to respond to their fears rather than trust God. However, that choice is costly every time. The Israelites feared the enemy and refused to believe

God, forfeiting their future in the Promised Land. Instead every Israelite over forty died in the desert (Numbers 14:22). Saul lost the kingship to David (1 Samuel 15:24-29). Peter began to sink when he feared the wind on the sea (Matthew 14:30). In each example, God gave someone a specific task but fear spoiled the victory.

I believe Luke 8:37 to be one of the saddest Scriptures in the New Testament:

> *Then all the people of the region of the Gerasenes asked Jesus to*
> *leave them, because they were overcome with fear.*
> *So he got into the boat and left.*

Imagine the eternal ramifications of the Gerasenes' fear! Jesus was ready to meet them, but their fear determined their destiny. Have you missed an encounter with Jesus out of fear? Have you refused a blessing offered by God to walk in a more comfortable direction? If so, describe your experience.

_____

_____

_____

_____

_____

If we are going to walk unhindered in wholehearted pursuit of Christ, we need to deal with our fears. What do we do when our circumstances are scary? What do we cling to when we are truly afraid? How can we ever live fearlessly?

ACTION STEPS

First, we can take the advice offered in Isaiah 30:19:

> *People of Zion, who live in Jerusalem, you will weep no more.*
> *How gracious he will be when you cry for help!*
> *As soon as he hears, he will answer you.*

We have the freedom to cry "Help!" It becomes our turn to trust He is big enough to take care of our scary situations. Sometimes I cry out in frantic, tearful frustration. It doesn't matter; He promises to hear me and answer me. Meanwhile, my job is to stop being afraid. Period. We need to stop playing the what-if mental tapes and stop thinking about all the legitimate reasons we have to be afraid. We need to stop letting fear hinder our wholehearted pursuits. Just stop it, and listen.

When God gives you an answer through His Word or encourages you not to fear, let this become your new mental tape. Jot it down and repeat it to yourself over and over again. Put it in a place you can see it until these words become such a part of your prayer life and your trips to Wal-Mart that you no longer need the note. The following verses are a great place to begin. Look at these encouraging words and complete the blanks:

Psalm 27:1. The LORD is my light and my salvation—whom shall I _____?

Psalm 56:3. When I am afraid, I put my _____ in you.

Psalm 56:4. In God, whose word I praise— in God I trust and am _____ _____.

Psalm 118:6. The _____ is _____ I will not be afraid.

My final suggestion for overcoming fear will not be popular. Think back to our list of biblical individuals who overcame fear. How did they do it? They did the very things that scared them to death. They recognized that the fears in front of them would impede them from something greater: obedience to God and the Lord Jesus Christ.

For many of us, trusting in His sovereignty and pressing through our fear is the crossroads of many a breakdown in our wholehearted pursuit of Christ. If that is you, as it is often me, let us ask the Father to make us different. Let us give Him the honest and ugly assessment of our fears, choose to trust Him, and walk in and through the very things that scares us. Will you commit to do this with me today? What will you trust Him with today?

_____

_____

_____

_____

_____

If you have it all together in the fear department, encourage those around you who do not. The body of Christ is in desperate need of encouragement and wisdom. Ask the Lord to bring to your mind someone who needs you. Write his or her initials in the blank. Then write two ways you could make yourself available and safe for that person to find courage in the Lord.

Who needs me?

_____

_____

How can I help?

_____

_____

Think about what hinders *you* from responding to God's love. Begin by asking Him to reveal anything that keeps you from living life to the fullest and loving Him with everything you are. Pray about or write down what you believe He is saying to you today.

_____

_____

_____

_____

_____

_____

_____

_____

_____

ENDNOTES

1. John D. W. Watts, *The Broadman Bible Commentary*, Clifton J. Allen, ed., (Nashville, Baptist Sunday School Board, 1969), 2:281.

2. Billy Graham, *The Holy Spirit: Activating God's Power in Your Life*, reissue ed., (Nashville: Thomas Nelson, 2000), 163.

NOTES

LESSON 2

WHEN HEARTS WAVER

Loving God is not so much something we do as something we become: Loving God is about being a twenty-four-hour, seven-day-a-week suitor of the Lord.[1]

My husband loves a home-cooked meal, like chicken potpie and my Ultimate Chocolate Cake, or roast and potatoes with carrot cake made from scratch. I don't understand it, but when I make a scrumptious dinner, the man feels loved, so I cook often. Cooking is not a chore because I love him and I know it communicates my devotion to him.

I enjoy drinking a Coke, especially when I'm writing—and Chad knows it. My hunk of a man strolls casually into my office with my favorite: a large half Diet Coke, half regular Coke—perfectly blended. (He has practiced it.) This surprise gift never gets old. He captures my heart all over again. Every time.

More than that you learn do's and don'ts for loving God with all your heart, mind, soul, and strength, I pray He will woo you closer to himself. As you spend time together, let Him speak love into your life in ways that are precious to **you**. Time and time again, the Lord will surprise me with words and tokens of love, similar to the exchanges I just described between Chad and me.

I was looking through a set of old sermons written by my favorite preacher, Charles Spurgeon, when a title—"*He Loved Us First*"—caught my attention because it was based on 1 John 4:19. When I turned to that sermon, guess what I discovered? Spurgeon preached it in 1883 on my birth date! I was moved to tears. I know that's quirky. You might not care anything about old books and has-been preachers. But this was on **my** birth date, by **my** favorite preacher, exactly *the* perfect sermon. In essence, this was God's way of bringing me a Coke. Not only does He totally dig me and all my weirdness, I think He was so delighted that I was seeking more understanding of His love that He gave me something meaningful that communicated **specifically to me.**

He woos us to himself; and grants us a supernatural capacity to love Him in return.

> Because He has invested Himself so heavily and materially
> within us through Jesus' death and resurrection and the subse-
> quent provision of the indwelling Holy Spirit, we have a super-
> human capacity to love Him.[2]

If you are thinking, *I want that,* keep reading. The King has been waiting for you.

If you are thinking, *I don't know what I want,* keep reading.
The King is patient. He will wait for you until you know.

If you are thinking, *That is exactly what I have*, keep reading.
The King has something special waiting for you.

If you are thinking, *I had that once, but I don't anymore,* keep reading.
The King has been expectantly awaiting your return.

Don't worry. God always makes the first move. But sometimes we stop reading. We allow our lives to be hindered from living life to the full. We continue our life of sinful choices. We settle for mediocrity out of fear. It feels impossible to believe God for what we cannot see. *Our hearts waver.*

For the next weeks of our study, we will study distinctions and learn vicariously through the experiences of others. Sometimes they get it right, like Hezekiah:

> *He did what was right in the eyes of the LORD, just as his father*
> *David had done.*
>
> 2 Chronicles 29:2

Other times they blew it. Take Jehoram, for example:

> *He followed the ways of the kings of Israel. . . (and) . . . did evil*
> *in the eyes of the LORD.*
>
> 2 Kings 8:18

Sometimes they got close, but not close enough. Remember Amaziah?

> *He did what was right in the eyes of the LORD,*
> *but not wholeheartedly.*
>
> 2 Chronicles 25:2

This week we focus on the latter two choices, those who wavered in loving God with all their hearts. *Lord, teach us today how to love you with all our hearts by showing us what it looks like **not** to.*

DAY 1

RELATIONSHIPS ARE LOST

If there was ever anyone equipped to love God with his whole heart, it was Solomon, raised by his father, David, "the man after God's own heart" (1 Samuel 13:14). Solomon had everything: the right environment, the right genes, an elite education, and a kingdom of his own. Promises were spoken over his life. Not only was he a very good Jewish boy, he was the **ultimate** Jewish boy, loved by God from birth (2 Samuel 12:24–25):

> *She gave birth to a son, and they named him Solomon. The*
> *LORD loved him; and because the LORD loved him, he sent word*
> *through Nathan the prophet to name him Jedidiah.*

 WALK IN THEIR SHOES

"Jedidiah. The giving of this name suggests that the LORD's special favor rested on Solomon from his birth. And since the name also contained an echo of David's name, it provided assurance to David that the LORD also loved him and would continue his dynasty."[3]

If that were not enough, God himself appeared to Solomon twice, giving him more than he asked for and telling him exactly what to do with his life. In spite of this ideal scenario, however, Solomon's heart eventually turned away from God:

> The Lord became angry with Solomon because his heart
> had turned away from the Lord, the God of Israel, who had
> appeared to him twice.

1 Kings 11:9

What went wrong? This is the tragedy of tragedies. We need to understand so we can avoid the same colossal mistakes. Tracing Solomon's life before he turned away will clarify this otherwise cloudy situation.

THE SETUP

Solomon was blessed with a father who spent his life pursing God's heart. Although David made huge mistakes along the way, his life was characterized by obedience and love for God. David modeled wholehearted devotion to God to his son. Blessings came to Solomon through covenant promises made to his father before he was even conceived. We learn God's plan for Solomon in Second Samuel. David voices concern that while he, a mere shepherd boy turned king, lived in luxury, it was not right for the Lord's dwelling place to be a measly tent. Read God's response to David's concerns, and underline every promise God makes to him:

> When your days are over and you rest with your ancestors, I
> will raise up your offspring to succeed you, your own flesh and
> blood, and I will establish his kingdom. He is the one who will
> build a house for my Name, and I will establish the throne of
> his kingdom forever. I will be his father, and he will be my son.
> When he does wrong, I will punish him with a rod wielded by
> men, with floggings inflicted by human hands. But my love will
> never be taken away from him, as I took it away from Saul,
> whom I removed from before you. Your house and your
> kingdom will endure forever before me; your throne will be
> established forever.

2 Samuel 7:12–16

God answered David's concern over His shabby quarters by pouring on more promised blessings. Solomon received a God-sized blessing years before he arrived on the scene: the assurance his kingdom would last forever and the unending love of God. It sounded too good to be true. But God is a giver. It is His character to give to His children.

Our lives in Christ are lavishly blessed as well. Read the following verses and write one sentence about what each of these promises means to you:

> Very truly I tell you, the one who believes has eternal life.

John 6:47

_____

_____

_____

*For I am convinced that neither death nor life, neither
angels nor demons, neither the present nor the future, nor
any powers, neither height nor depth, nor anything else in all
creation, will be able to separate us from the love of God that is
in Christ Jesus our Lord.*

Romans 8:38–39

_____

_____

*For we are God's handiwork, created in Christ Jesus to do good
works, which God prepared in advance for us to do.*

Ephesians 2:10

_____

_____

David instructed Solomon on how to accomplish what God had chosen him to do. David understood the heart of God enough to know these instructions were conditional. **Not** following God's instructions would bring dire consequences. Read 1 Chronicles 28:8–10. What would happen if Solomon chose to love God with all his heart? If he didn't?

_____

_____

God's call to live in wholehearted devotion to Him continues today. Do you understand He has loved you too—since before you were born? Do you know His promises to you? Are you familiar with how He has equipped you as a believer? What does 2 Peter 1:3–8 tell you about your ability to accomplish all God plans for you when you love Him with your life? What if you choose **not** to?

_____

_____

_____

THE BEGINNING

Solomon began his reign on a firm foundation. Not only had wholehearted pursuit been modeled for him, and not only had promises been spoken over him, but his God-given roles and responsibilities had been plainly explained. If this were not enough, after the dedication of the temple, God himself appeared to Solomon, giving him the opportunity to ask for whatever he wanted!

*At Gibeon the LORD appeared to Solomon during
the night in a dream, and God said,
"Ask for whatever you want me to give you."*

1 Kings 3:5

How did Solomon respond (vv. 7–9)?

_____

_____

_____

God was pleased with Solomon's request and He gave him blessings Solomon **DIDN'T** ask for— peace from enemies, long life, riches—in addition to what he did ask for (vv. 10–13).

Often what we want more than anything speaks volumes about the state of our hearts. Solomon demonstrated his heart for loving the Lord by asking for what he desperately needed to do what God called him to do.

Jesus gives us that same freedom and opportunity! Read Matthew 7:7–11. Today, what you would request?

_____

_____

_____

If your love for God could be measured on a continuum based upon what you ask for—whether you are thinking merely about personal gain or thinking about Him—where would you place yourself?

Self-centered love   _God-centered love_

James warns about our requests reflecting our hearts:

> _When you ask, you do not receive, because you ask with wrong_
> _motives, that you may spend what you get on your pleasures._
>
> James 4:3

The human condition is that of self-centeredness, which is why Solomon's request pleased God. It was God-centered, rather than self-centered. Solomon felt the weight of the responsibilities set before him and his own deficiencies to shepherd God's people, and he asked for help. The mark of those who love God with all their hearts is when their deepest desires reflect God's will for their lives.

If I am ever going to love God with my whole life, my desires must align with His plan and His dreams for me. My heart needs to be purified from everything else:

> _Therefore, since we have these promises, dear friends, let us_
> _purify ourselves from everything that contaminates body and_
> _spirit, perfecting holiness out of reverence for God._
>
> 2 Corinthians 7:1

Write a prayer to the Lord today. Tell Him the condition of your heart and what you believe to be His desire for your life. Ask Him to mold your desires to reflect Him more and more.

_____

_____

_____

_____

_____

_____

Despite the good start Solomon had, his single-minded attraction to God began to waver toward worldly gain and softness toward sin. We will see how his heart became divided and his beautiful early relationship with God was lost through a series of choices. We will need to look introspectively at our own paths to ensure we do not follow Solomon's example, no matter what the cost.

DAY 2

KINGDOMS ARE FORFEITED

Solomon knew the promises, the expectations, and the tender love of God, but over time he lost sight of these and ultimately chose to look in the opposite direction. The grandeur of the kingdom Solomon ruled was lost, together with the intimacy he shared with God. Make no mistake: the kingdom wasn't forfeited overnight. Neither did Solomon's love for God grow cold with one shocking incident. Solomon's journey away from wholehearted love for God was no different than the journey we can find ourselves trekking. How seriously God considers this conditional relationship is sobering. He allowed David's son—the one He loved (2 Samuel 12:24), the one of promise, the handsome and formidable one who had everything he could possibly desire—to lose it all, pointing God's people in the opposite direction and leaving a deplorable legacy. God will not force us to love Him back. Today, let us press up against the scriptural glass as we learn from a venture none of us ever wants to travel.

THE QUESTIONABLE MARRIAGE

Solomon's best-known wife was the daughter of Pharaoh (1 Kings 3:1). However, the heir to the throne was Rehoboam, whose mother was an Ammonite woman named Naamah. We don't know when Solomon married Naamah (1 Kings 14:21), but it would have been just as he began to reign. Solomon was king forty years (1 Kings 11:42), and Rehoboam became king at age forty-one (1 Kings 14:21).

What was the problem with marrying Naamah? Solomon's sentiments exactly! Although marriage to Ammonites was not specifically forbidden in the law as it was with other neighboring people groups, the law speaks of them, clearly defining relationship parameters:

> *No Ammonite or Moabite or any of their descendants may enter the assembly of the LORD, not even in the tenth generation.*
>
> Deuteronomy 23:3

> *Do not seek a treaty of friendship with them as long as you live.*
>
> Deuteronomy 23:6

In this scenario, Solomon took the letter of the law rather than the *spirit* of it. *"Hey, the law doesn't say I can't marry her. I just can't sign a friendship treaty with her. Or take her to church."*

Is it OK to do that? The Bible does not address each and every circumstance we face. If we want to honor God and love Him with all our hearts, what should we do when a situation like this one pops into our lives?

Read Matthew 5:27–28. What does Jesus' response tell us about how He might view Solomon's choice?

_____

_____

Sometime I have a choice to make that Scripture doesn't specifically address. Like Solomon with his the-law-doesn't-say-I-CAN'T-marry-her rationale, I am often tempted to pursue the choice I want because no chapter and verse specifically condemns it. Have you heard this line of reasoning before? Rarely do people want to justify spending money on the poor, sticking it out in their marriage, or giving their time at a pregnancy crisis center. Usually the choice deals with getting as close to sin as possible and getting away with it. This is a slippery slope we have all treaded, one that leads us away from God's heart.

This is serious business if we want the full-life promise. What decisions have you faced that have tempted you to follow the *letter* of the law as Solomon did rather than the *spirit* of what the law intends?

_____

_____

_____

This dangerous ground is a familiar temptation for "good Christian girls." What should we do? First, we need to stop and pray it through. The right course of action for Solomon would have been to pray, "Lord, may I marry an Ammonite woman? The law is not clear." Sometimes, godly counsel is in order. We should always put ourselves in God's Word. More often than not, just as in Solomon's situation, the answer to my dilemma is there—I simply choose not to see it. But to love God with all our hearts requires us to be receptive to His instruction and obedient to follow through with whatever He says.

Often, the Word of God is straightforward, leaving no excuse for misunderstanding His instructions. Long before there was a kingdom to rule, God laid out for Moses what was to be expected in the king who would rule His people. Read Deuteronomy 17:14–20 and check which of the following instructions were given specifically to kings:

He must not acquire great numbers of horses or chariots.

He must not send people back to Egypt for any reason.

He must not take many wives.

He can marry anyone he wishes.

He must not acquire large amounts of silver and gold.

He must write the law, keep it with him, and read it.

He must follow the law carefully.

Solomon slipped from wholehearted devotion to complete disregard for obedience to God's commands during the first twenty years of his reign. We can see this in several areas of his life.

THE QUESTIONABLE MILITARY STRATEGY

Solomon strengthened his kingdom by collecting hoards of chariots and horses (1 Kings 10:26) as well as making alliances with other nations (1 Kings 3:1). Among politicians, such actions might be considered shrewd. God sees things differently.

Solomon knew the law, and he *chose* to break it. He strategically strengthened himself rather than relying on God. He had the resources to buy the chariots and horses. What could it hurt to store them up for a rainy day?

In the days of bad economic conditions and warnings of recessions, the temptation to supply all we might need is real. When you have the means to hoard, how much is enough? How much money should remain in our retirement accounts at the expense of today's great kingdom needs? What is too much and becomes sin? These are questions we all must wrestle.

In 2 Samuel 8:4, David faces similar issues, and in Luke 12:22–31 even Jesus speaks to this. In your own words, describe how these verses might shape *your* decisions.

_____

_____

_____

The key is to rely on God for all our needs and to keep our hearts tender to His whispers that say, "That is enough. Rely on me, not on yourself. Give the rest away."

THE QUESTIONABLE EXTRAVAGANCES

Not only did Solomon disobey God by collecting large amounts of gold and silver, he cultivated an affinity for personal extravagance. What does 1 Kings 7:1 convey that might represent a red flag about Solomon's devotion to the Lord over himself?

_____

_____

Jesus shared a parable that serves as both a warning and a guide. Read Luke 12:13–21. This passage contains what author Randy Alcorn calls the Treasure Principle.[4] Jesus says that while we cannot take our earthly wealth to heaven with us, we can send it there ahead of us. The warning is to not set our hearts on material things: *stuff*. The instruction is to instead be *"rich toward God."*

How can you and I send wealth ahead by being rich toward God?

_____

_____

_____

_____

Is it wrong to possess wealth? Yes and no. To truly possess and clench our fists around what we have is wrong. A. W. Tozer offers Abraham as an example: "He had everything, but he possessed nothing. There is the spiritual secret."[5] Wealth is not wrong, but it is dangerous. It will either keep our hands open and our knees to the ground in submission to what God desires, or it will rob from us the fullness of life both now and for eternity. In Luke 12, Jesus finishes His teaching on material wealth with these words:

> For where your treasure is, there your heart will be also (v. 34).

What is the state of your heart in regard to stuff?

_____

_____

_____

LOVE REDIRECTED

Sometimes God is gracious enough to issue a warning, or at least a second chance to straighten up. At the end of twenty years, God appeared to Solomon a second time and instructed him to walk in *"integrity of heart and uprightness"* (1 Kings 9:4). If he did, God would do everything He promised. If not, there would be serious consequences.

Consider this Solomon's "come-to-Jesus meeting": that personal, in-your-face, it's-time-to-make-a-choice-**or-else** sort of meeting. (I've held several, usually with my children when I have put up with as much as I'm going to endure.) My meeting might sound like this: "If you don't cut it out, I am about to snatch you bald-headed!" They get the point and change their behavior.

Read 1 Kings 9:2–9 aloud. It reads like a come-to-Jesus meeting. This appearance did not come right after the beautiful ceremony and temple-consecration prayer when God responded with a consuming fire and an engulfment of the Spirit (2 Chronicles 7:1–3). Instead, I think God was losing His patience. But being rich in mercy, God humbled himself and appeared before the same person a second time. What is your takeaway from this meeting?

_____

_____

Solomon did not change course. In fact, it is after this second meeting we read the death knell of his heart condition:

> King Solomon, however, loved many foreign women besides Pharaoh's daughter—Moabites, Ammonites, Edomites, Sidonians and Hittites. They were from nations about which the LORD had told the Israelites, "You must not intermarry with them, because they will surely turn your hearts after their gods." Nevertheless, Solomon held fast to them in love. He had seven hundred wives of royal birth and three hundred concubines, and his wives led him astray.
>
> 1 Kings 11:1–4

With a wayward heart comes wayward behavior. Read 1 Kings 11:7–10. The worship of these two false gods signified how far from the Lord Solomon had strayed. Such worship required the sacrifice of children, often the firstborn. Solomon also supported the worship of Ashtoreth (1 Kings 11:33), a fertility goddess, which involved sexual relations between the worshipers as well as the priests and priestesses. The list of offenses toward God in the worship of idols piled up under Solomon's leadership.

Solomon was a good Jewish boy: loved by God, filled with promise, equipped for every good work. But sin covered the landscape of his heart. The same can be true of "good Christian girls." *Secret sin. Socially acceptable sin. Halfhearted sin.* These begin to fill the landscapes of our hearts until there is no room for Him. Not only do we lose the beautiful relationship, but often the loss extends beyond ourselves.

THE FORFEIT OF A KINGDOM

Within forty years, the kingdom that once boasted of magnificence and singleness of heart stood in moral ruin, never to return to its former glory. Here is the climax of our vicarious experience with Solomon: his downfall was not one isolated misstep but a series of choices to lean into sin, striving toward the line of sin he could get away with. Over time, the severity of sin increased until his heart turned away.

The road away from wholehearted devotion is marked by sin progression. I pray for an amplified sensitivity toward sin. If you are participating in behaviors you know are sinful, I pray you get caught. I pray for second appearances through the Word to take root in our lives. But more than anything, I pray that the road toward loving God with our whole hearts is clearly marked, so that we might not drag His name through the mud behind our own. His name is worth more than my sinful choices. I pray He is worth more than yours.

DAY 3

HEROES NEVER MATERIALIZE

God's call to wholehearted pursuit and fruitful living is not limited to kings with perfect backgrounds and life handed to them on a platter. He calls regular people, like you and me, to God-sized tasks. Today our focus turns to those who were given the opportunity for greatness but refused to heed the call or welcome the challenge.

SOMETIMES WE FORFEIT THE OPPORTUNITY

Barak received a call from God but gave up the opportunity. During the period before the kings, when God appointed various individuals to serve as judges over the people, Deborah received a word from the Lord concerning Barak. She sent for him and he came before her. Read Judges 4:6–7. What did Deborah say would happen to the commander of Jabin's army?

_____

Can you imagine? God is ready to turn this regular guy into an instant hero whose tale of victory would be told through the ages. All Barak needs to do is show up. Instead, he acts like my girls going to the restroom at a restaurant:

> *If you go with me, I will go; but if you don't go with me,*
> *I won't go.*
>
> Judges 4:8

I believe Barak suffered from more than a juvenile uncertainty of self. He responded out of a twisted belief that God could work through someone like Deborah but not through him. This inaccurate assessment of God's ability to greatly use a regular guy cost Barak his distinction as a hero:

> *"Certainly I will go with you," said Deborah. "But because of the course you are taking, the honor will not be yours, for the LORD will deliver Sisera into the hands of a woman."*
>
> Judges 4:9

Why was God offering this honor to Barak in the first place? We don't know. Maybe God had more planned for Barak *after* Sisera's defeat that required an experienced hero. Maybe He wanted to reveal himself more to Barak through the victory. Maybe God was simply being generous to a regular guy who had done nothing to deserve it. We will never know, because Barak refused to embrace the opportunity.

David trusted God to equip him for great challenges. Read 2 Samuel 22:36. What did David say God did for him when he was faced with hero-defining moments?

_____

_____

When was the last time you felt you were less than God's treasured possession? When have you sensed God could use someone like *her* (some other person) but not plain, ordinary, mistake-ridden you?

_____

_____

When was the last time you dismissed a nudge toward something beyond your ability or for which you were completely unprepared, believing there was no way God would ask you to pursue *that* task?

_____

_____

Let us not forfeit the opportunity to become heroines because we disbelieve God's ability to give us His shield of victory and His willingness to stoop down to make His name great through us.

SOMETIMES WE HAVE OUR OWN BLUEPRINT

Like Solomon, Jeroboam was handed everything he needed for success. Unlike Solomon, he was an unlikely candidate for greatness. Read the account of God's plan for Jeroboam in 1 Kings 11:26–39. What was God giving him, and why?

_____

_____

_____

_____

I find it interesting that God chose to give the majority of His people to an obscure leader, much like God's choice to hand over the enemy to a regular guy named Barak. Jeroboam was nothing particularly special, just a man with a propensity for leadership and hard work.

Circle the conditions for all these great promises to be accomplished:

> *If you do whatever I command you and walk in obedience to me and do what is right in my eyes by obeying my decrees and commands, as David my servant did, I will be with you.*

> 1 Kings 11:38

Sound familiar? God had offered a similar promise to Solomon, in person. This time the message was delivered through the prophet Ahijah, who specifically spelled out when this amazing turn of events would occur. Underline the conditions required for Jeroboam to inherit the kingdom:

> *But I will not take the whole kingdom out of Solomon's hand; I have made him ruler all the days of his life for the sake of David*

*my servant, whom I chose and who observed my commands
and statutes. I will take the kingdom from his son's hands
and give you ten tribes.*

1 Kings 11:34–35

Look again at 1 Kings 11:26. What tells us trouble was brewing before the kingdom was transferred to Jeroboam?

_____

Scholars believe the rebellion was treason because it was an act serious enough to cost Jeroboam his life (v. 40):

*Solomon tried to kill Jeroboam, but Jeroboam fled to Egypt, to
Shishak the king, and stayed there until Solomon's death.*

At different times, God told both Jeroboam and David that they would be the next kings. Read 1 Samuel 26:8–10. Then write the differences between David's actions and Jeroboam's.

DAVID	JEROBOAM

While Jeroboam heard God's plan for his life, he seemed to want to help Him accomplish the plan *right then,* putting his cart before his horse. I know someone else who does that too: *me.* I know all too well how this works: I think I have received a specific word . . . so I begin working all the angles to bring it to pass. (At least I'm in "good" company. Abraham's Sarah did the same thing when God promised an heir, introducing Ishmael into the world, and ultimately the Islamic religion along with him).

Loving God with our whole hearts requires having patience to wait for God to move. We submit to His timing. Scripture contains the memo I always miss:

*The LORD is not slow in keeping His promise,
as some understand slowness.*

2 Peter 3:9

The choice to rebel is a heart issue. We want God's promise *now.* We fear that if we wait we might miss the blessing, or maybe this great thing will never happen. We think, *I'd better act now, before it's too late.*

The truth is, just as for Barak, our fear of forfeiting our blessing while we wait on God's timing is misplaced. God will not give your hero-making moment to another unless you refuse to believe Him. Even then, I've known Him to be gracious. Many times I have waited for God to do what He said He would do, only to lapse into discouragement, questioning my ability to hear Him. This is not what Jeroboam was doing. He was taking the blessing prematurely by force. As one commentator assessed, *"He had no right to seize what God has promised to give."* [6]

Jesus faced a similar test. Read Matthew 4:8–9. What do you think was Jesus' actual temptation?

_____

_____

Describe a time when you were tempted to manipulate a situation (or a person) in order to "help" God.

_____

_____

When have you felt God's timing to be slower than it should be?

_____

_____

Choosing **not** to await God's perfect timing—attempting to orchestrate His blessing ourselves—is always disastrous. When Solomon eventually died, everything changed within a matter of days. Solomon's son Rehoboam acted upon advice that convinced the majority of people to reject him as king, inadvertently facilitating Jeroboam's ideal opportunity—just as God promised. Read 1 Kings 12:20. The prophecy became Jeroboam's reality. Had this given Jeroboam reason to trust God with his new kingdom responsibilities?

> *Jeroboam said in his heart, "Now the kingdom will return to the house of David."*
>
> 1 Kings 12:26, AMP

However, when Jeroboam perceived problems on the horizon, instead of relying on the Word of God, he forged his own path. Unfortunately, that progression of heart-to-thought is familiar to me too. I lose sight of what God said, exaggerating my challenges through my "life lenses." Overwhelmed with a sense of urgency to act, I start thinking **my way** is the only solution. This is where heroes are lost, and this is exactly what happens in 1 Kings 12:28–33.

Jeroboam's next moves first shipwrecked the nation, then tainted *fifteen* kings who reigned after him! All of them committed "the sin of Jeroboam," heresy. The thing that became known as "the sin of Jeroboam" is rooted in the picking and choosing what you are going to believe, honor, and uphold and throwing the rest out the window.

> *Heresy is defined as the arbitrary selection of doctrines or practices or a choosing—instead of dutifully accepting those which God has enjoined.[7]*

Jeroboam missed his calling to greatness by seizing what God had promised to give before it was time for him to receive it. What if he had waited for God to move, rather than rebelling and being forced out of the country? What if he had prayed to God, asking how he could be obedient to His word in this difficult and divisive situation? What might Israel have looked like—in power, in blessing, in unity—if Jeroboam had properly ruled all that his heart desired?

Unfortunately, we will never know because he missed his opportunity. Jeroboam is a hero who never materialized.

Complacency Prevails

Tea parties are one of my girls' favorite activities. They often invite me. While sometimes we use real food, most of the time we settle for plastic. Regardless, I pretend to eat what I'm served. As I move the cookie toward my mouth, giving the illusion of chewing, eight-year-old Zoe grabs my hand just in time and says, "Mommy, don't eat it! We are just pretending the cookies are real!" as if I cannot tell the difference between shiny plastic and an actual Oreo®. Just as lucidly, God can discern when we pretend our hearts are completely His. Today's study illuminates this uncanny ability, inspiring us to live beyond make-believe.

HOPE AMID BRAZEN REBELLION

Yesterday we left Jeroboam with a kingdom that eventually came to moral, religious, and governmental ruin. Over time, God was simply no longer willing to accommodate Jeroboam's blatant disregard for God and the people's sinfulness. The Assyrian army conquered Israel in 722 BC, scattering its people abroad, never to be united again.

The smaller kingdom, Judah, remained intact for almost a hundred years following Israel's exile. This kingdom was blessed with several kings who served God wholeheartedly. The final one was Josiah, during whose reign we can see two significant events important to our lesson today. Read the following verses and describe what happened:

2 Chronicles 34:8, 14–19

_____

_____

_____

Most scholars believe the book was Deuteronomy. The effects of the law on King Josiah were profound.

Chronicles 34:29–33

_____

_____

_____

With a total heart transformation, Josiah initiated a series of reforms based upon the rediscovered law He experienced. However, at this point, the people were entrenched in sin. They believed they could simply perform the outward acts of ritual and sacrifice and God would bless them. Their hearts, however, remained unchanged.

It was at this exact point in history that God spoke to His people through the prophet Jeremiah. Read Jeremiah 3:6–10 and fill in the blanks:

> "In spite of all this, her unfaithful sister Judah did not return to me with _____ _____ _____, but only in _____," declares the Lord.

> Jeremiah 3:10

The people pretended to repent. They confessed. They brought their offerings and sacrifices. They celebrated the Passover. But because the temple was in the center of the city, they believed God would never allow Jerusalem to be captured by their enemies. They believed they could pretend to eat the cookie and God would never know the difference.

HEARTS UNMASKED

In the following verses, identify God's pulse on the human heart:

Psalm 44:20–21: God knows _____ of the heart.

Proverbs 21:2: God _____ the heart.

Jeremiah 17:9–10: God _____ the heart.

Let us not be fooled into thinking there is no pretense among us to love God with all our hearts. Some believe

"If I give my money, or help with Bible school I will look like I love God with my all."

"If I go to Bible study and condemn what I am expected to condemn and approve of what is right, nobody will know about my hidden addiction."

"If I smile a lot, get everyone here by bribing them, and put on my perfect-life church face, no one will suspect it's not authentic. Then I can go home and get back to the real me."

The reality is we are great pretenders.

THE CANDOR OF GOD

The Lord was on to the make-believe world of His people. He recognized the shiny plastic imitation:

> *My people have committed two sins: They have forsaken me, the spring of living water, and have dug their own cisterns, broken cisterns that cannot hold water.*
>
> Jeremiah 2:13

Too often I read the words of Scripture without emotion. I forget God is real and that He feels everything we feel. "The heart of God is no figure of speech, but a reality. It rejoices in our love, it mourns over our sin."[8] Read Jeremiah 2:13 again, but this time, sense God's rejection and brokenheartedness over His beloved's choices.

Today thousands of man-made cisterns in Upper Galilee remain. Experts suggest that "at best they are an uncertain source of supply, and the water, when collected, is bad in color and taste, and full of worms."[9] So goes our make-believe Christianity. We pretend our relationships are authentic, vibrant, and satisfying—but we know our cisterns are broken and full of worms, leaving us empty, more alone, and more defeated than ever. Could it be we have forsaken Him to build our own versions of God complete with shiny plastic cookies?

Take this opportunity to examine your heart. Have you dug your own cisterns? Have you been trying to keep your life together, hoping no one will discover your leaks? Pursue authentic repentance. Don't move a step further. Choose the Oreo.

_____

_____

_____

_____

_____

OUSTING COMPLACENCY

When I was a little girl, my dad was pastor of a Southern Baptist church. One Sunday afternoon, just before our mission class started, another girl and I decided to play Hide from the Teacher. Turns out, we had more stamina for hiding than she had for seeking. The teacher went home in tears, and I received a stern lecture from my mother regarding higher expectations. Somehow my friend escaped unscathed. That day I learned the difference being the preacher's kid makes.

Judah was held to a higher standard than Israel—and found wanting. Unfaithful Judah is actually worse than faithless Israel. God expected more, as He should have. They knew better. They had the priests, the prophets, the temple, and the very **words of God**.

If you are reading this, He expects more. Why? Because you know better! You've lived longer. Some of you have probably *taught* this concept. Are you living it out? Maybe you even speak fluent Christianese, but your heart has wavered. Maybe you have fallen into complacency, offering Him less than, well . . . **all**.

He expects more because you are in a relationship with Him, and He loves you. Jeremiah 4:3–4 tells us what to do when we have rejected the spring to embrace our own worm-infested cisterns:

> This is what the Lord says to the people of Judah and to Jerusalem: "Break up your unplowed ground and do not sow among thorns. Circumcise yourselves to the Lord, circumcise your hearts."

What does this mean? Resolve to be yielded to God. No matter where you are on the continuum of wholehearted pursuit, "Have done with insincerity," says one theologian. "Hypocrisy is hateful."[10] Allow God access to throw up some dirt on that dormant surface so long unmoved. He says to us, "Stop wavering." Stop considering options other than total heart surrender, or the fulfillment of life will be choked out.

Lord, may we be done with make-believe tea parties and worm-infested water. Quench our thirst with the limitless refreshing spring only you can give us. We give you our broken attempts to satisfy ourselves with our own versions of you. Stir up the dirt of our hearts, even if it hurts. Refill our empty places with your perfect love.

Day 5

OPPORTUNITIES ARE SQUANDERED

The past decade of my life has been filled with questions about how to live out the Greatest Commandment. The single motivating factor inspiring me to continue taking each new step is the dread of being less than everything God created me to be. I don't want to miss anything. I don't want to finish my life, stand before the Lord, and be confronted with what **could have been.** You and I have one opportunity to get this right. God forbid that we waste it. John Piper came to this conclusion:

> If I wanted to come to the end of my life and not say, "I've wasted it!" then I would need to press all the way in, and all the way up, to the ultimate purpose of God and join him in it.[11]

That is your invitation today: press all the way in—and all the way up! Discover more fully the purpose of God for your life, and choose to join Him in it. Come in close. Read Mark 10:17–27. Do you believe the young man was sincere in his quest for eternal life? Justify your response.

_____

_____

_____

Other Gospels call this man the rich young ruler. Most scholars believe this man desperately sought an audience with Jesus. Look at how he approached Him. This distinguished gentleman *ran*. He ran to Jesus, who was leaving, not wanting to miss his opportunity. Consider also his humility. He was a well-to-do, highly educated, well-respected superior—falling on his knees before a poor, uneducated inferior (in all religious standings), a carpenter's son from Nazareth. Somehow, this rich man understood that Jesus was different than how He appeared, and he refused to allow pride to cause him to miss his opportunity.

What do you think the rich man expected Jesus to say?

_____

_____

This unnamed rich man can remarkably resemble us at this point in the narrative. He knows the law. He reads Scripture. He serves. He gives. He loves. He walks the straight and narrow road away from sin. If he had been lying or embellishing his religious track record, Jesus would have called him out in his hypocrisy. The rich man truly loves God . . . but not **wholeheartedly.**

Loving God like this man did is still a wasted life. Yet we often do love God like him, squandering opportunities to experience the richness God has prepared for us, not seizing our hero-making moments. Our problem is one of the heart.

John Piper describes an example of how we emulate loving God like this young man today:

> *Oh, how many lives are wasted by people who believe that the Christian life means simply avoiding badness and providing for the family. So there is no adultery, no stealing, no killing, no embezzlement, no fraud—just lots of hard work during the day, and lots of TV and PG-13 videos in the evening (during quality family time), and lots of fun stuff on the weekend—woven around church (mostly). This is life for millions of people. Wasted life. We were created for more, far more.*[12]

This young ruler recognized his need for more. He ran to Jesus. He fell down before Him and asked the big question of life, but he didn't receive what he expected. While he asked the big question, he was in no way ready for the big answer. His religion was more outward observance than spiritual dependence. He was not prepared "to subordinate all, to surrender all, to sacrifice all, and to suffer all, if necessary, in fulfillment of that Law, the whole of which is contained in that one word, love."[13]

I believe Jesus knew this about him. Seeing through his heart condition, what was Jesus' immediate response to the man (v. 21)?

_____

Beautiful! Always, no matter how lacking we are when we fall before Him, **He loves us first.** To me, these words are the most important. Without them, Jesus simply issued another burdensome command. Even as I write this, my tears flow. *He loves us first!*

Only after Jesus loved him did He answer the question:

> *"One thing you lack," he said. "Go, sell everything you have and*
> *give to the poor, and you will have treasure in heaven.*
> *Then come, follow me."*

Mark 10:21

Make no mistake. Clearly, this man's life was proof of his committed love for God. Jesus did not go around requiring everyone to sell their possessions and give the money to the poor. It was required of *this* man in particular because Jesus saw his heart: "**One thing** you lack."

If you had Jesus' attention today, and He said these words to you, what is your "one thing"? Is there something you are holding tight-fisted in your life? What stands between you loving God with **most** of your heart and loving Him with **all** of it?

_____

_____

_____

_____

_____

Jesus did not tell the young man exactly what the one thing was. Instead, He told him what was necessary to surrender himself completely. Something in his wealth, whether it was comfort, safety, honor, or pleasure, insulated him from absolute commitment to God.[14] In essence, Jesus was saying to him, "This wealth is standing between you and Me. Don't keep it. It's not worth it. I promise I can restore all of this and more in eternity. Trust Me. Give it away, and follow Me."

While I was studying for this lesson, my husband and I had the privilege of giving a generous gift to someone close to us. They needed to receive it as much as we needed to give it. We want open hands when it comes to managing the resources God has entrusted to us. Openhanded giving has been our practice. But this was a sizeable gift, and giving it initially caused me more reservation than it did my spouse. However, I do not want to clench my fist around what I have, so I willingly agreed to release it with an open hand. We made the offer, and when it was graciously and humbly received, my heart was glad.

About a week later, we learned that the generous gift was not going to cover the expenses. An *extravagant* gift was needed. We didn't have the resources to be that extravagant, but this reality did not negate the leading to give. Being as transparent as I know to be, my heart reaction was similar to that of our main character today:

> *At this the man's face fell. He went away sad,*
> *because he had great wealth.*

Mark 10:22

My heart was no longer glad. It was anxious. As I prayed about what we should do and waited for His answer, I felt the Lord whisper in my spirit, "Cheri, right now, this is a heart issue. Yes, I want you to have open hands, but I also want your fingers spread apart as far as possible. Let my provision sift completely through your hands. Don't squander the opportunity to live out what I am teaching you. Do not lack anything! Resist stopping short of loving me with all your heart for something as insignificant as money."

Jesus' call to give everything away mystified the rich young man. He walked away, unchanged and unyielding. We have that same opportunity to miss. Anything we choose to clench our fists around keeps us from greatness, just like the rich young man. As far as Scripture tells us, he missed his chance. He squandered his opportunity for greatness.

But what if he hadn't?

> *Who can tell what might have been the effect of his sacrifice?*
> *His example might have saved Judas. He might have enriched*
> *the world with a fifth Gospel. He might have drawn many of the*
> *rulers to believe. But for the time he lost his chance,*
> *and the world is the worse for his decision, as it is the*
> *worse for every error of men.*[15]

Now it's your turn. What will you decide? Press all the way in. Climb all the way up. Come in close to what He is teaching you about loving Him with your whole heart. Seize the opportunities God is bringing you. Don't miss a single hero-making moment! Use this space to pour out your heart to Him.

_____

_____

_____

_____

_____

_____

_____

_____

_____

ENDNOTES

1. George Barna, *Think Like Jesus: Making the Right Decision Every Time* (Nashville: Integrity, 2003), 104.

2. Ibid., 104.

3. Note on 2 Samuel 12:25, *Zondervan NIV Study Bible* (Grand Rapids: Zondervan, 2002), 442.

4. Randy Alcorn, *The Treasure Principle* (Sisters, OR: Multnomah, 2001).

5. A. W. Tozer, *The Pursuit of God* (Camp Hill: Christian Publications, 1982), 27.

6. A. Rowland, *The Pulpit Commentary*, H. D. M. Spence, Joseph S. Exell, eds., (Grand Rapids: Wm. B. Eerdmans, 1962), 5:247.

7. J. Hammond, *The Pulpit Commentary*, H. D. M. Spence, Joseph S. Exell, eds., (Grand Rapids: Wm. B. Eerdmans, 1962), 5:275.

8. S. Conway, *The Pulpit Commentary*, H. D. M. Spence, Joseph S. Exell, eds., (Grand Rapids: Wm. B. Eerdmans, 1962), 11:34.

9. D. Young, *The Pulpit Commentary*, H. D. M. Spence, Joseph S. Exell, eds., (Grand Rapids: Wm. B. Eerdmans, 1962), 11:44.

10. Conway, *The Pulpit Commentary*, 11:90.

11. John Piper, *Don't Waste Your Life* (Wheaton: Crossway, 2007), 28.

12. Ibid., 119–120.

13. J. J. Given, *The Pulpit Commentary*, H. D. M. Spence, Joseph S. Exell, eds., (Grand Rapids: Wm. B. Eerdmans, 1958), 16:105–06.

14. Henry E. Turlington, *The Broadman Bible Commentary*, Clifton J. Allen, ed., (Nashville: Baptist Sunday School Board, 1969), 8:349.

15. Ibid., 88.

LESSON 3

WHEN HEARTS HOLD NOTHING BACK

Last week my two teenagers and I shopped for a semiformal event they would be attending. The dresses had to fit their bodies as well as our budget and stay within the enforced dress code. We searched two weeks and two cities before we succeeded, but the girls were stunning the night of the event.

This week, we are on the hunt once more. We are shopping formals, but this time, our shopping destination is Goodwill. Taylor and Addison are attending a church youth function called *Thrift Store Prom*. Each girl finds the most outrageous dress she can (within the dress code); then they all rock out to Christian music at our local skating rink. The event is hysterical, but contrasted with the previous event, it causes me to reflect on my own choices.

Does anyone besides me want the fairy tale, with the Savior riding the white horse, swooping down to pick you up, adorned in a royal gown made specifically for you? I desperately want the King to be enthralled with my beauty—inside and out. I want to forget my people and my father's house—that which keeps me hindered from receiving His love and giving mine in return. Yet each day when I have the choice to put on the thrift-store dress or the genuine royal gown with my name on it, too often I play dress-up. I continue to live a hindered life. I forget His goodness and provision for me, I disbelieve His words, and I **settle** for the thrift-store dress because I'm not sure the royal gown will fit. Yes, the thrift store variety will do, so I hold back.

If you are even a smidgen like me and yearn to know the God who loves you more than you can fathom with such convincing authenticity that it changes the way you live, then it's time for both of us to *stop holding back*. Instead, we need to receive His love by choosing the life we've been given, and begin to return our affections with a little more gusto, a little more trust, and a little less hesitation.

This week, let's begin to lessen the death grip we have on our own hearts. Find your special place. Pour your favorite coffee. Wear a pretty dress, just because He loves you, and sit down before Him. The fairy tale is real. He has been anticipating time with you. Today, you and I will begin to see how to love Him with all of our hearts, holding nothing back.

DAY 1

INHERITANCES ARE GAINED

Recently all eight of our children spent the night at Mema's house. Go ahead and gasp—it's appropriate! Finagling all eight is a lot for one person, so it doesn't happen often. Making the transition of authority, we gave the normal threats-and-expectations speech and left the kids in grandma's hands.

Apparently this was not a blissful experience. The speech landed on deaf ears with most of the little ones. Only two of the six youngest followed our instructions. Those who closed their ears were given the opportunity to experience the Strange family version of a little activity we call Shock and Awe: Shock because they did not realize we would find out or how well we know them (and can administer punishments that ensure a change in their behavior), and Awe because the two who listened were given a weekend with Mema all to themselves (equivalent to a day at Disney World!). The expressions on the faces of the others were priceless. They had no idea THAT reward was an option. Truthfully, it wasn't. We had a point to convey. I am certain, next time, all ears will be hearing properly.

I wonder if God was administering a little Shock and Awe of His own as He dealt with Caleb and the unbelieving Israelites:

> But because my servant Caleb has a different spirit and follows
> me wholeheartedly, I will bring him into the land he went to,
> and his descendants will inherit it.

Numbers 14:24

Caleb is the first person Scripture identifies specifically as one who followed God wholeheartedly. Caleb's character and love for God didn't spring up overnight. What does Numbers 13:1–6 disclose about him?

_____

_____

We might assume Caleb was an elder in the clan, given that role by default. Because he lived in a society that honored patriarchal leadership, we might be tempted to skim over the list and move quickly to the action of the story. However, two realities should cause us to pause:

1. Caleb was not an elder. He was young, a mere forty years old (Joshua 14:10).

2. Caleb had an unusual heritage (Numbers 32:11–12).

Caleb's father, Kenaz was an Edomite. Who were the Edomites? Read Genesis 36:9, 11.

_____

Caleb associated himself with the tribe of Judah, but these were not his relatives. Nonetheless, he lived in such a way that he became a leader among the people of God. These spies chosen were younger men because of the physically taxing assignment, but they also were "men of position and repute."[1] In a society in which family was everything, Caleb was an unlikely candidate for wholehearted seeking because he was not even a part of God's chosen people, Israel. Because of his family heritage, it would be impossible for him to gain an inheritance in the Promised Land.

That option was not even on the table for discussion.

OPPORTUNITIES FOR FAILURE

More than these cards stacked against him, Caleb had several opportunities to fail to love whole-heartedly that impacted the rest of his life as well as the lives of his descendants. We can learn a great deal from such an unlikely candidate.

HE COULD HAVE SHRUNK BACK

Read 2 Timothy 1:7 below.

> *For God did not give us a spirit of timidity (of cowardice, of craven and cringing and fawning fear), but [He has given us a spirit] of power and of love and of calm and well-balanced mind and discipline and self-control* (AMP).

What kind of spirit have we been given through Christ?

_____

_____

Suppose Caleb had said, "No, thank you, I'm not qualified. You'd better look somewhere else"? Does this reasoning sound familiar? Has there been (or is there currently) a time when you believe God asked you to do something that you were (technically) not qualified to do? Could you think of at least two other people who were *more* qualified, *more* gifted, and *more* equipped and ready than you? Naturally, you shrank back? You might have believed it was a sign of humility to let someone else go into that place of responsibility (even though God nudged *you*). If that describes your situation, you might need to know that the word "timidity" is translated from the Greek, *deilia,* which means "cowardice."[2]

The same *spirit*[3] (Greek, *rûah*) that made Caleb recognizably distinct from the others, setting him apart, is the same *spirit*[4] (Greek, *pnuema*) that Paul writes about to Timothy. Shrinking back, or being too timid or shy to walk forward in the responsibility God calls us into, is *not* humility. It's failure—failure to love Him wholeheartedly.

The enemy wants nothing less than to steal our absolute and uncompromising affection for God. He can snatch it right out from under our noses before we realize it. Caleb stepped up and took hold of the responsibility given to him, in spite of his heritage and the normal cultural expectations.

What about you? Do you tend to walk forward in the responsibilities God has given you or to shrink back in timidity? How can you walk resolutely toward God's purposes for your life?

_____

_____

_____

When I married, I borrowed a wedding dress from a cousin. We didn't have the money to be extravagant, so our wedding was simple. Very much was the loan appreciated because I needed a dress and it looked lovely, but *I knew* it wasn't mine. Have you ever felt that you were in some-one else's dress—that it wasn't really for you? You probably walked with timidity. You may have stood less confidently. A few years ago I realized I was living spiritually as if I were still wearing my cousin's dress.

This young man, Caleb, was not even an Israelite! He had no reason to risk anything. He would not receive an inheritance. You could say that he wore someone else's clothing. Yet somehow Caleb saw the love of God clearly and experienced Him as his own, in spite of who he was. He figuratively took off the borrowed robe of Judah he was wearing and put on the one God made for him, to walk in bold courage.

When I began to catch a small glimpse of what you read here today, I did something very frivolous and out of character. I took my saved mad money and found someone to custom design a wedding dress. Just shy of twenty years into my marriage, I bought a wedding dress. It was *my* dress, made to *my* measurements, perfectly fitted for me.

> *She has been permitted to dress in fine (radiant) linen,*
> *dazzling and white—for the fine linen is (signifies, represents)*
> *the righteousness (the upright, just and godly living, deeds, and*
> *conduct, and right standing with God) of the saints*
> *(God's holy people).*
>
> Revelation 19:8, AMP

Almost twenty years after I was married, I put on my dress, had my hair done, and my family and I spent the afternoon with a photographer. The pictures taken that day hang prominently in our home. When I look at them, I see a confident daughter of the King. There is poised a woman choosing to put on a royal gown—the dress that was made for *her*. I do not need to borrow anything. The timid little girl in the cousin's dress is no more. My God is my King, completely enthralled with the radiant beauty his righteousness brings at any age. *There is no need to shrink back.*

Caleb did not shrink back because he was an Edomite rather than an Israelite. Even though he was a descendant of Esau, he stepped up and put on his royal robe because he had a different spirit—one that loved wholeheartedly. We have been given the same spirit.

Is it time you too take off your cousin's dress? You might be an unlikely candidate for wholehearted pursuit, but there awaits a beautiful gown, custom made to your specifications. What is a first step you can take toward wearing the spiritual dress made for you?

_____

_____

Is there something visual you need to set in motion, like my late photo op with my family? It's not silly if it will help you make spiritual progress.

_____

_____

_____

HE COULD HAVE HELD HIS TONGUE

Read Numbers 13:26–29. The majority of the spies reported that the land was exactly what God promised it would be, with the exception of the big scary dudes with the incredibly fortified cities. Then before they could continue with their fear mongering, Caleb took center stage. This was his defining moment. Read Numbers 13:30 and write his suggestion below.

_____

_____

_____

_____

God's decision to bless Caleb resulted from his willingness to speak on His behalf. Sometimes you and I get worked up about things that are not our responsibility. We think about situations for hours and develop all sorts of solutions to problems we have not been appointed to solve. But sometimes God burdens us with a word He wants spoken. How can we tell the difference?

See Proverbs 3:1–35. If you can prayerfully work through those verses with the sense that your motivation is pure and you continue to have the nudging that God is leading you, then ask yourself these three additional questions:

1. Is this word consistent with Scripture?

2. Does this word magnify God and reflect His character, or does it magnify me?

3. Am I in the relational position to speak it boldly as I should in love?

> *"Where God's command is clear, our wisdom is to venture upon great things for God, and to expect great things from God."*[5]

HE COULD HAVE JOINED IN THEIR CONTEMPT

Read Numbers 14:1–11. The Israelites believed they had endured enough. Their decision to select a new leader and kill the ones God selected stretched beyond unbelief—they had cultured an utter disregard and disdain for God. Therefore they preferred stoning Moses and Aaron rather than meet the challenges ahead.[6]

 WORD STUDY

The word "contempt" in Numbers 14:11 is translated from the Hebrew word nāʾaṣ, which means "spurned; despise, revile."[7] The Complete Word Study Dictionary in its definition for this word expounds further: "This word [nāʾaṣ] often refers to rejecting the counsel of a wise person" suggesting a scornful attitude. "Another example of a passage that uses this word is Proverbs 1:30, where wisdom laments that people scorn her reproof. In another instance of this word, the Israelites were chastened because they had rejected God's Law (Isa. 5:24)."[8]

Caleb could have been tempted to save his own skin, to allow his voice to fade into the clamor of the other spies by conceding, "You're right. What was I thinking? I was simply trying to be encouraging in an impossible situation. Forget it." But somehow Caleb overcame that temptation and sided with the leadership about to be overthrown and killed. Can you imagine? He stood before the assembly to remind them about God's goodness and ability to bring them victoriously into a good land, and for his testimony the hordes were ready to kill him. He honored God at the risk of his life.

> *"God does not lead his people into temptation, but he does call them to pass through the tempering fires of stress. He does not do this to break them but for the righteous to have the opportunity to demonstrate what they really believe."*[9]

God does not need our help to defend His honor, but He is glorified and pleased when we do. There is blessing in resisting our opportunities to fail. Like my two kids who did not realize obedience at Mema's house would lead to privilege, Caleb never could have anticipated the lavish gift

God gave him. He was a descendant of Esau—not of Jacob. The Promised Land did not apply to him. That is the outrageousness of Caleb coming into an inheritance all his own:

> *Because my servant Caleb has a different spirit and follows me wholeheartedly, I will bring him into the land he went to and his descendants will inherit it.*
>
> Numbers 14:24

Caleb could have missed the Promised Land. Instead, he **lived in it.**

You and I have the promise of life to the full and the Spirit to equip us to love God wholeheartedly. We too can enter our inheritance and begin living in it.

How does Caleb's life example speak to you today?

_____

_____

_____

DAY 2

HINDRANCES ARE DEFEATED

Loving God with all our hearts is first and foremost a spiritual matter. Like Caleb, David had opportunities to fall short of loving God with all his heart and settle for mediocrity. We can be thankful that Scripture provides us with a rich array of examples for learning how to become women after God's own heart by studying the habits and choices that characterized the man after God's own heart. Today's lesson follows David in his hindrance-defying moments and teaches us how to defy our own.

DAVID CONSIDERED SIN TO BE SERIOUS BUSINESS

According to Psalm 19:12–13, what concerned David?

_____

_____

If only we were as wise in our prayers of confession as David in this psalm! He rightly perceives he may not recognize where he has gone wrong and asks for forgiveness over these areas. However, he also understands he is sometimes a willing participant in sin to the extent that his sin controls him. From this sin he also prays for release. How different could we live day to day if we would concentrate on these two areas of confession?

If you were to follow David's example, what would be your prayer?

_____

_____

_____

_____

DAVID BELIEVED GOD

Paramount to David's success in walking unhindered was his resoluteness to simply believe God. When God gave instructions, David did not falter in unbelief. We do not find him in a puddle of tears, complaining about how awful the situation seemed or how impossible the circumstances appeared. Instead, he consistently relied on God for direction. Look at 1 Samuel 23:1–5. What was the question posed by David, and how did God respond?

_____

_____

_____

I relate to David's men wanting certainty about God's answer. David did exactly what he should: he asked the Lord *again*. God's answer remained the same, so in spite of their fear, David and his men walked forward in obedience.

Last year, just before we brought home our four children from Ethiopia, my husband was offered a different job. It was very appealing because it would allow him to work regular hours. He would partner with a friend, and we would not need to relocate. It sounded perfect. However, as we prayed and looked to God's Word for direction, the answer was no, and Chad turned down the job.

A few months later, he was asked to reconsider. We felt silly, but again, we prayed: "Lord, we heard your answer. We accept your authority and trust you. But we have been asked to consider this job again. We trust you to speak to us, and whatever you say, we will do." This time the answer was yes. Because the answer changed in our situation, I was afraid to move forward, much like David's men. I wanted confirmation. As we waited for Him to answer, God was faithful to speak in ways we could understand, just as He was for David and his men. Chad resigned the next week.

David took his problems, questions, and calamities to God in prayer, believing He would speak to each specific situation:

> Trust in him at all times, O people; pour out your hearts to him,
> for God is our refuge.
>
> Psalm 62:8

He will do the same for you. What are you seeking God about in this particular season of your life?

_____

_____

Another aspect of faith that sets David apart is his tenacity in believing God could and would fulfill His promises. David was anointed king as a young man, long before he would begin to reign. However, he waited for God to work. He did not help God with the situation even though he had opportunities to move the timeline along (1 Samuel 24, 26). It was only when Saul's life ended in battle against the Philistines that David petitioned God about the promised kingship. In 2 Samuel 2:1–4, what does David ask?

_____

Paramount is what David **did not** ask. He did not ask *if* he was ever going to become king. He did not whine and pout about how long it had been since he was anointed king. Nor did he assume authority over the situation, as did our friend Jeroboam. He simply assumed he *would* be king, based upon the promise of God. He waited and allowed God to be God, asking only whether the time had come. I love that. Actually, this one stings quite a bit.

How many times have you asked God the wrong questions at the wrong times? When was the last time you walked like David toward God's promises over your life? How might you need to inquire differently to demonstrate your own tenacity to believe God is faithful?

_____

_____

_____

Before we move on, where did God send David to become king (vv. 1, 4)?

_____

Is there anything you find interesting about His choice? Read Joshua 14:13–14.

_____

_____

DAVID REFUSED TO FORGET

David did more than play defense against the enemy. One of the most powerful offensive tools David utilized to seek wholeheartedly was his refusal to forget, not only from where he came but also the utter and absolute faithfulness of God.

In 1 Samuel 17:32–37, what does David refuse to forget?

_____

Therefore, what is he able to do (v. 50)?

_____

What is something you need to remember about God that will help you defy the temptation to forget His ability to pull you through your current situation?

_____

_____

DAVID WAS RELEASED FROM FEAR

A fourth hindrance that could have easily sidetracked David in his pursuit of loving God with all his heart was fear. David had plenty of opportunities to allow fear to overpower obedience, but he conquered fear in a way we can emulate. Psalm 3:1–8 shows us how.

1. Run to God and blow the whistle on your enemies.

> LORD, *how many are my foes! How many rise up against me!*
> *Many are saying of me, "God will not deliver him."*
>
> Psalm 3:1-2

2. Ask God to take care of it.

> But you, LORD, are a shield around me, my glory, the One who
> lifts my head high.

Psalm 3:3

> I lie down and sleep; I wake again, because the LORD
> sustains me. I will not fear though tens of thousands assail me
> on every side.

Psalm 3:5-6

3. Let God deal with the scary stuff.

> From the LORD comes deliverance.
> May your blessing be on your people.

Psalm 3:8

God alone conquers fear. Do you need to run and lay bare what is keeping you terror-stricken? Do you need Him to take care of a frightening situation? What burdens your heart today? He does not leave you to navigate life alone.

_____

_____

_____

_____

_____

DAY 3

WE ARE FREE TO LOVE

> Shake off your dust; rise up, sit enthroned, Jerusalem.
> Free yourself from the chains on your neck, Daughter Zion,
> now a captive.

Isaiah 52:2

Let me remind you, we are walking this journey together. In fact, you may be miles and miles ahead of me in many respects. At times it feels as if a chasm separates David's heart and mine. Take, for instance, this morning's verbal exchanges, *not* a picture of perfection. I am still learning to recognize the potholes, obstacles, and detours I must maneuver to live a life unhindered. Yet the man after God's own heart did **more** than avoid hindrances; **he loved freely**. Unlike David, I'm keenly aware how often I do not.

My tendency is to hold back. Not only must I overcome a personality that is more similar to a wallflower than the social butterfly, but life has taught me the safety of keeping my emotional cards close. Be selective with love. Keep the boundaries between others and yourself clear. Put on a warm smile and show great interest in the other person, yet build the emotional wall high and thick. But holding back is not Christ's purpose for me:

In [this] freedom Christ has made us free [and completely lib-erated us]; stand fast then, and do not be hampered and held ensnared and submit again to a yoke of slavery [which you have once put off].

Galatians 5:1, AMP

To become a woman who loves God with all her heart, I must release myself from the chains of lesser love that bind me. Today's lesson is for girls like me who will begin to know the depths of God's heart only when we experience the freedom to love.

BY SINCERE CONFESSION

Psalm 32:1–5 describes a particular type of experience for David. According to these verses, what is he going through?

_____

_____

My daughter Addison drinks deeply of fun and life. When she was very young, this trait I so enjoy today displayed itself in remorselessness. Regardless of the punishment, Addison believed get-ting in trouble was worth it. She would look at me undaunted and without emotion. One day my confident, strong-willed four-year-old walked sheepishly down the stairs (which was unusual), and began crying (also unusual). Then this precious little girl led me upstairs to find where she had attempted to scale the drapes in her sister's room. She had failed about halfway up the wall. Now the drapes and the bent rod, blinds, and debris lay scattered across the floor.

Normally, I would have been furious. But this time I did not worry about the destruction. My remorseless daughter was upset that she had done something wrong! For the first time in her life, she was miserable because of her sin.

David approached God about his sin in a similar manner, as if it broke his heart. He gives the picture of groaning and wasting away, with emotional turmoil sapping his strength. Tender hearts that love deeply mourn over disappointing someone dear. Like my Addison, who took me upstairs to show me her error, David did not try to cover up his sin before God.

What was God's response (v. 5)?

_____

Consider what David did as a result: he moved on to bask in the love and character of his God who forgives freely (vv. 1–2). He did not continue to act as if he had never been forgiven. He moved forward.

We keep ourselves chained to lesser love when we refuse to move on. Imagine Addison emotion-ally carrying forward the burden of pulling down the drapes those years ago. Suppose she kept it front and center in our relationship: "Mom, I'm still so sorry for what I did. I know you loved those curtains. I know I messed up terribly. I'm sorry. I'm sorry. I'm sorry." How ludicrous. You might say, "But Cheri, you don't know what I've done." No, I don't. I do, however, know what David did. He committed adultery and then he tried to cover it up; when that didn't work he committed murder (2 Samuel 11). If you have committed sins equal to the gravity of David's, emulate him.

Blessed (happy, fortunate, to be envied) is he who has
forgiveness of his transgression continually exercised upon him,
whose sin is covered.

Psalm 32:1, AMP

Has there been (or is there currently) any circumstance or situation in your life in which you can follow David's example through sincere confession and the courage to move on?

_____

_____

_____

THROUGH CONFIDENCE IN THE LORD

Another contrast between the man after God's own heart and, well, the rest of us, is found in David's complete and utter confidence in God. He not only trusted God, he believed God is who He says He is. David lived out in his reality what he believed as his theology. Wouldn't we turn our world upside down if we could just do the same?

The psalms are replete with David's outpouring of his confidence. In David's heart (what he thought and believed) and in his experience, God comes through every time. Read Psalm 103. List five benefits David found in trusting his God.

1.

2.

3.

4.

5.

In addition to the benefits found in Psalm 103, other psalms record reasons for placing confidence in God. Star the three that speak the most clearly to you today:

Psalm 6:9 _____God hears my cry and accepts my prayer.

Psalm 28:7 _____He is my strength and shield.

Psalm 31:19 _____The Lord is good.

Psalm 33:4 _____He is faithful.

Psalm 34:4 _____He delivered me from all my fears.

Psalms 41:2 _____The Lord protects.

Psalm 54:7 _____He has delivered me from all my troubles.

Psalm 57:2 _____He fulfills His purpose for me.

Psalm 63:7 _____He is my help.

Psalm 139:1 _____God knows everything about me.

Locate the three verses you marked, writing the word *If* in front of the phrase. At the end of the phrase, write the word *then* and fill in what should go next. Mine might read like this:

Psalm 57:2 *If* He fulfills His purpose for me, ***then* I can trust His timing when it feels like He is late.**

WITH GENUINE THANKFULNESS AND PRAISE

David attained all God had promised—above and beyond what he could have imagined—in power, wealth, and standing, yet he never lost sight of who he was in relation to God. Instead of becoming prideful and arrogant, David remained thankful. He expressed his gratitude without restraint while maintaining a high view of the giver. We see his attitude throughout the psalms as David calls on the people to share his thankful heart and sing praises to God.

Finish the following verses from the book of Psalms:

Psalm 7:17. I will give thanks to the LORD because _____ _____ _____; I will _____ the _____ of the name of the LORD Most High.

Psalm 28:6–7. Praise be to the LORD, for he has heard my cry for mercy. The LORD is _____ _____ and _____ _____; my heart trusts in him, and he helps me. My _____ leaps for joy, and with my song I _____ him.

Psalm 105:1–2. Give praises to the LORD, _____ _____ _____; make known among the nations what he has done. Sing to him, sing praise to him; _____ of all his wonderful _____ .

Psalm 106:1–2. Praise the LORD. Give thanks to the LORD _____; his love endures forever. Who can proclaim the _____ _____ of the LORD or fully declare his praise?

Sometimes the temptation to read these as surface exchanges and religious platitudes enters my mind. A person who wallows in mediocrity can still sing praises and express gratitude. What sets David apart from everyone else?

An encounter between David and the Lord, recorded in 2 Samuel, sheds light on what added to David's distinction as a man after God's own heart.

Read 2 Samuel 7:1–3. What about David's statement to Nathan gives us a clue into the genuineness of his love for God?

_____

_____

Summarize God's response in verses 5–16.

_____

_____

_____

_____

Imagine David thinking about all the goodness God has shown him and wondering what he could do for God in return. It's as if the very consideration of the inequity of the situation—*the man* living in a palace while *the God* is living outside in a tent—opened the floodgates of God's abundance. David never saw it coming and was completely overwhelmed (vv. 18–21). However, I imagine God, sitting on the edge of His throne, longing to burst this word upon Nathan: "David—because your heart reflects my own—what I'm about to do for you is so incredible, you are going to have to take a seat!"

I will sing the Lord's praise, for he has been good to me.

Psalm 13:6

WITHOUT RESERVATION

Now the man who danced before the Lord with all his might just a chapter before (2 Samuel 6:14) makes sense. David could not help himself:

I will become even more undignified than this, and I will be humiliated in my own eyes"

2 Samuel 6:22

It's not simply his personality. He was just a shepherd boy—an unimportant ragamuffin. Yet with the Spirit upon him, his unswerving concern for obedience, and the passion required to love God with all his heart, David is able to love freely: without guilt, filled with awe and thankfulness, in absolute confidence, without reservation.

Was David perfect? No. We've already noted his sin with Bathsheba and the orchestrated murder of her husband, Uriah the Hittite (1 Samuel 11). We also have biblical testimony of the poor parenting job he performed with his own children—for example, how he handled his daughter's rape by her brother, the murder of said brother by another brother, and the kingdom swiping by his son Absalom (1 Samuel 13–14). No, David was most definitely **NOT** a portrait of perfection. However, if the *process* is the point, David succeeded. In his pursuit of the God he loved, he succeeded wholeheartedly. May God move us to seek Him more passionately and love more freely because of this flawed example who loved God without holding back.

In what ways is God moving you to love more freely? How can you loosen your grip on your heart today?

_____

_____

_____

DAY 4

CHANGES ARE REQUIRED

Remember the sermon preached on my birth date that I mentioned last week? Published in the late nineteenth century, the books belonged to my grandfather, who served as a Baptist minister for fifty years. The set was given to him by a pastor from the previous generation. They were in the possession of my father as he ministered, and now they belong to me.

I hold three college degrees from Baptist institutions; and I began my marriage as a third-generation pastor's wife. You could say I have a heritage rich in the Word of God and the equipping to proclaim it.

Some of you do not share the privilege of a Christian heritage. You may be like my friend Tracy, the first in her entire family lineage to follow Christ. Or maybe you are one of the few in your family who acknowledges faith in Christ. Maybe you are from a family of believers who, like Solomon's grandson Abijah, share this testimony:

He committed all the sins his father had done before him; his heart was not fully devoted to the Lord his God, as the heart of David his forefather had been.

1 Kings 15:3

Regardless of what has come before in your life, you can make the choice to live differently. You can turn your generation and the ones that follow *toward* wholehearted pursuit. You can be the one to break the chain of halfhearted devotion, leading the way toward loving God with all your heart. Our next example under the spotlight will show us how.

Read 1 Kings 15:9–11. What is the testimony in Scripture regarding the next king?

_____

_____

The life of Asa is a powerful example because we don't really know why he chose to follow God as David had done. It certainly was not based upon a positive family heritage. Yet he made the choice to stop walking in the same direction his family had walked and courageously chose God. Whatever the cause, Asa had quite a lot of work to do. For those of you waiting on a list of how to jump-start wholehearted living, Asa created one.

CHANGE REQUIRES A GOOD CLEANING

The story of Asa is found two places in the Old Testament. Locate both passages and leave something to mark them: 1 Kings 15:12–15 and 2 Chronicles 14:2–6. Using these two passages, list elements of change instituted by Asa's commitment to serve the Lord wholeheartedly.

• removed the foreign altars

•

•

•

•

•

ⓘ DID YOU KNOW?

Were the high places were removed? Bible commentators agree the high places were likely shrines built similarly to Canaanite altars but used exclusively for the worship of the Lord in remote locations.[10] *The problem with these sites was that they contradicted the Word of God in worship and sacrifice to Him (Deuteronomy 12:2–7). Scholars believe it is probable Asa ordered the removal of the high places, but this was easier said than done, especially out in the countryside.*[11]

Housecleaning like Asa displayed is something to do in our own lives as we move toward wholehearted pursuit. It's likely that some things need to go! If you are paving a new way in your life or family, your to-do list may look a lot like Asa's. If you have been serious about following God most of your Christian journey, ask God to reveal what needs cleaning. Ask Him to give you wisdom about what is keeping you from loving Him with all your heart today. He will.

In fact, recently I entered my house, said a couple of things about a couple of people I shouldn't have said, and walked out remorseful, asking God's forgiveness. It was a sinful act, spurned out of a sinful habit. What I said wasn't awful. It's not as if my mouth is filled with filth. That has never been the temptation. Sometimes I say things that are *acceptable* in the halls of Christian mediocrity but **NOT** acceptable for those desiring to love God completely. There is no room for it here. I'm packing up the habit and throwing it out. And I will need to continue to work through this cycle—thinking about what I say and hesitating before I speak—until this habit has no hold on me.

Take time to pray about your own life and habits. What may God want you to throw out? Use the space below as needed. I'll be ready to move on when you have finished.

CHANGE REQUIRES RISK

We learn a bit more about the reign of Asa in Second Chronicles. Read 2 Chronicles 14:8–15. What did Asa do that demonstrated his heart to follow the Lord, and what was God's response?

This was a hindrance-defeating moment! Asa had a choice to make. Was he going to seek the Lord or rely on other means against the enemy? In this particular instance, Asa walked unhindered, refusing to forget who God is and what He can do. He articulated his own frailty as well as God's power. This is exactly what we saw David do yesterday. God is faithful to deliver.

CHANGE REQUIRES HELP

Let's move to 2 Chronicles 15:1–8. In these verses, we are introduced to Azariah. Describe Azariah's role in this passage.

Interestingly, the name Azariah appropriately means "The Lord has helped."[12] When Asa heard these words and the prophecy of Azariah, he took courage. Change can be exhausting, with slow-appearing results. Even the courage to continue with what God desires can leave us winded. Azariah met Asa with the exact inspiration and encouragement needed to do what God called him to do. This passage can do the same for you and me. How does verse 7 meet you in your need today?

Encouraged by Azariah, Asa removed the detestable idols and repaired the altar in front of the temple. Now continue reading verses 9–15. Three things are noteworthy in this section.

1. Change Becomes Contagious.

People came over to Judah from Israel because the Spirit of one who wholeheartedly pursues God draws others to himself (v. 9). How does this example relate to the words of Jesus in Matthew 5:14–16?

_____

_____

_____

2. Change Marks Lives.

We live in a culture lax on covenant. Let's face it, commitments are restrictive, and the decision to preserve personal freedoms and opportunities is championed. We observe this reality through divorce rates and the choice not to marry but to cohabitate. In fact, we even prefer phones and cable connections without contracts, and many churches have dismissed the membership option altogether. Our culture has forgotten the liberating effect of promise keeping.

A serious commitment to seek the Lord wholeheartedly, as seen with Asa, gives life and vitality to personal pursuits as well as to corporate worship experiences. Here we see it used to draw the people of God to a more serious pursuit of God. What if you made a written promise to do the same and devised a plan to keep your commitment? What if your study group organized a commitment ceremony, on a voluntary basis, to seek the Lord wholeheartedly, following these weeks together? If this option is unavailable, what if you joined with me through an online commitment (www.cheristrange.com)? Of course, there will be mistakes made along the way (by all of us), but you and others in a group could join together in a greater pursuit than the standard Christian satisfaction of waddling through puddles of mediocrity. What are your thoughts about this possibility?

_____

_____

_____

_____

_____

3. Change Leads to More Difficult Change.

Deposing grandma was a courageous but possibly heart-wrenching move on the part of Asa. Here he demonstrated a reckless abandonment to God over sinful and destructive family ties. Grandma not only worshiped idols but fostered the practice.[13] The king removed grandma from her influential position. He took her idol, stomped on it, crushed it (much like Moses crushed the golden calf), and burned it at the Kidron Valley, where the sewage of the temple ran. The queen mother's idol worship was detestable to God. It could not be overlooked simply because it resided with someone dear.

Asa is not alone in experiencing difficult family relations. There are no easy answers, for sure. One thing we can learn from Asa is to align our words and actions with the truth of Scripture. Paul calls us to hate what is evil (Romans 12:9). Jesus instructs us to forgive others as God forgives us (Matthew 6:12). He instructs His disciples to live in such a way that they are recognized for their love of one another (John 13:35).

We often stop with love and forgiveness, for mastering these are epic challenges. Yet Jesus speaks further about how His followers are to relate to one another. Read Luke 12:49–53; 14:25–27. How might these words of Jesus impact our relationships that require the kind of courage Asa displayed in his rightful dealings with sin and wholehearted love of his God?

_____

_____

_____

You might want to close your time today with a prayer similar to mine:

Dear Jesus, I long to be different. I simply find change too painful to endure. Show me the way. Bring me encouragement (in human flesh and bones, if possible, as you did for Asa). Increase my zeal to follow truth, and give me wisdom to deal with each difficult relationship. Thank you for your constant pursuit of me and your unashamed advances in wooing me closer and closer to yourself all the days of my life. It's working. . . .

DAY 5

RELATIONSHIPS FLOURISH

Today as I write this lesson, I am expecting a gift from my husband. It will not be diamonds or anything expensive, but it will be a personal gift. We have been married over twenty years. He knows my affinity for gifts. According to *The Five Love Languages* by Gary Chapman[14] my love language is giving and receiving gifts. If you want to show the love to Cheri Strange, give her a present!

This revelation has been a key discovery in our marriage. Because Chad knows I receive love through gifts, he takes the time to pick something out and spends the money to purchase it. He also gives me the freedom to buy him gifts, even when he does not need anything. Learning how Chad and I exchange love has allowed our relationship to blossom and flourish over the years. Investigating how God receives love may be just as freeing in your relationship with Him.

DISCOVER WHAT LOVE LOOKS LIKE

If we were to take our cues from Scripture, focusing on the relationship between the Father and the Son, how do you believe God receives love?

John 12:49–50

_____

John 14:30–31

_____

Philippians 2:5–8

_____

Succinctly stated, "Christ emptied himself in order to be filled up with obedience."[15]

I can think of several other things I would like to be filled up with rather than obedience. (At the moment, M&M's® would be at the top of my list). Herein lies my problem. As Philippians describes, Jesus understood best how to love God with all His heart. He knew His purpose and fulfilled it completely. I struggle with this combination.

In the following Scriptures, how does Jesus communicate the secret to loving God and living out one's purpose?

Luke 11:27-28

_____

John 14:15

_____

John 15:9-10

_____

If God had a love language, what would it be?

_____

In addition to what we learn from Jesus, the Son, how does Acts 13:22 distinguish David as the man after God's own heart?

_____

Our willingness to do what God desires is a crucial element to loving God with all our hearts. This call can be found in most books of the Bible. Many individuals failed to heed the call. Most chose their own way. But if we want to become passionate followers of Jesus, obedience is imperative.

In your own life, if obedience is the measure of your love for Jesus, where would your love reside on a scale of 1 (being little love) to 10 (being absolute love)?

1   10

Is Jesus a broken record on this topic, or does He simply understand my yearnings for M&M's® over obedience? Why the frequent parallel between love and obedience? How will my obedience enable my relationship with the Lord to flourish?

OBEDIENCE INSTRUCTS OVER TIME

My efforts to shed light on my own ponderings brought me to Exodus 13:17-18:

> When Pharaoh let the people go, God did not lead them on the road through the Philistine country, though that was shorter. For God said, "If they face war, they might change their minds and return to Egypt." So God led the people around by the desert road toward the Red Sea.

What if the **process** is entirely the point? Suppose God is more concerned with the *journey* marked out for each us than the final destination? If this is accurate, He would want the relationship to be marked by *learning to love* Him in response to His love to us. But (and here is where my candy bowl overpowers me) we are not like Him. Instead, we are impatient to arrive at perfection. We don't want to wait to grow and learn. We have no interest in serving our desert time and taking the long road. Like the Israelites, we want to be in our promised lands or back in Egypt. No, the prospect of the **process** being the point is not appealing.

Think of what the newly freed Israelites would have missed: crossing the Red Sea on dry land, water gushing from rocks, daily manna, and the display of God's glory on the mountain. What if God wants to demonstrate and disclose himself in ways that only take place in the process of learning to love Him completely? He *could* make us godly through our pillows overnight. That route would indeed be shorter. But that is not His style. Instead, He woos us through a dynamic, growing love relationship all the days of our lives.

OBEDIENCE DEVELOPS ATTENTIVENESS

On the long route toward the Promised Land, God held daily exercises in obedience: in daily provisions with manna (Exodus 16:4-5) and in daily decisions with the cloud leading them (Exodus 40:36-38). How might God's dealings with the wandering Israelites relate to the words of Jesus in John 10:1-5?

_____

_____

_____

OBEDIENCE BECOMES PLEASURABLE

Jogging is an activity I have enjoyed since I was fifteen. I run several times a week. Chad and I have even finished a couple of marathons together. Last month we went away for the weekend to rest and celebrate my birthday. We ran six miles and treasured every minute. Jogging is not burdensome now. I have learned the discipline it requires and experienced its benefits. Jogging is a part of my life, and when I do not have time for it, I long to run.

Compare Matthew 11:28-30 and 1 John 5:3-4. Think about the words of Jesus spoken for our benefit. Realize that John the apostle is writing his words as an older man with lots of experience following Christ under his belt. What do these verses communicate about the work of obedience? How do we experience obedience to the one who loves us most in such a way that it becomes more pleasurable than my yearnings for M&M's?

_____

_____

_____

Finish your week of study in prayer. Ask God to help you loosen your grip around your heart to begin loving deeply and freely. Tell Him of your desire to have a flourishing relationship with Him, and allow Him the freedom to show you how and when to follow. Hold nothing back, my friend. He is much more satisfying than any other yearnings.

_____

_____

_____

_____

_____

_____

_____

_____

_____

_____

ENDNOTES

1. R. Winterbotham, The Pulpit Commentary, H. D. M. Spence, Joseph S. Exell, eds., (Grand Rapids: Wm. B. Eerdmans, 1958), 2:143.

2. Edward W. Goodrick & John R. Kohlenberger III, Zondervan NIV Exhaustive Concordance (Grand Rapids: Zondervan, 1999).

3. Ibid.

4. Ibid.

5. W. Binnie, The Pulpit Commentary, H. D. M. Spence, Joseph S. Exell, eds., (Grand Rapids: Wm. B. Eerdmans), 2:160.

6. Ronald B. Allen, The Expositor's Bible Commentary, Frank E. Gaebelein, ed., (Grand Rapids: Zondervan, 2012), 2:817.

7. Goodrick & Kohlenberger, Zondervan NIV Exhaustive Concordance.

8. Warren Baker & Eugene Carpenter, The Complete Word Study Dictionary Old Testament: OliveTree Bible Software edition (Chattanooga, TN: AMG Publishers), definition for Strong's Hebrew #5006.

9. Allen, The Expositor's Bible Commentary, 817.

10. John H. Traylor, Jr., Layman's Bible Book Commentary (Nashville: Broadman, 1981), 6:37.

11. Clyde T. Franscisco, The Broadman Bible Commentary, Clifton J. Allen, ed., (Nashville: Broadman, 1970), 3:381.

12. Traylor, Layman's Bible Book Commentary, 122.

13. T. Whitelaw, The Pulpit Commentary, H. D. M. Spence, Joseph S. Exell, eds., (Grand Rapids: Wm. B. Eerdmans, 1962), 6:191.

14. Gary Chapman, The Five Love Languages: The Secret to Love That Lasts, (Chicago: Northfield, 2010).

15. Robert B. Hughes & J. Carl Laney, Tyndale Concise Bible Commentary, "Philippians," (Bible Explorer 4 software, WORDsearch, 2007).

LESSON 4

WHEN MINDS SHORT-CIRCUIT

My y mind is my primary battlefield in life: the crossroads of decision making, my thinking can push me off course or drive me toward a more intimate relationship with God. I can persuade myself into wasting my life away through limited and trustless musings. Truthfully, if I allow myself to follow the kinds of thought patterns we will study this week, I am no more than two weeks from a faith catastrophe. My mind is powerfully connected to whether I love God with everything I am. Chances are, you and I are very much alike.

Jesus understood the struggle we would encounter and gave himself as the remedy, as the apostle Paul wrote:

> For I know that good itself does not dwell in me, that is, in my sinful nature. For I have the desire to do what is good, but I cannot carry it out. . . . So I find this law at work: Although I want to do good, evil is right there with me. For in my inner being I delight in God's law; but I see another law at work in me, waging war against the law of my mind and making me a prisoner of the law of sin at work within me. What a wretched man I am! Who will rescue me from this body that is subject to death? Thanks be to God who delivers me through Jesus Christ our Lord!
>
> Romans 7:18, 21–25

Not only has God rescued us and provided the power to overcome our unregenerate thinking (1 Corinthians 2:16), but Jesus made sure He was clear in communicating our responsibility to love Him with all our thoughts and attitudes (Mark 12:30):

> Love the Lord your God with all your heart and with all your soul and with all your mind and with all your strength.
>
> Mark 12:30

WORD STUDY

The Greek word for *heart* refers to the seat of thought and emotion. The heart was believed to be the seat of the inner self (composed of life, soul, mind, and spirit). In the New Testament, it takes on many aspect, including "(a) the set of physical life, Acts 14:17; James 5:5; (b) the seat of moral nature and spiritual life, the seat of grief, John 14:1; Rom. 9:2; 2 Cor. 2:4; joy, John 16:22; Eph. 5:19; the desires, Matt. 5:28; 2 Pet. 2:14; the affections, Luke 24:32; Acts 21:13; the perceptions, John 12:40; Eph. 4:18; the thoughts, Matt. 9:4; Heb. 4:12; the understanding, Matt. 13:15; Rom. 1:21; the reasoning powers, Mark 2:6; Luke 24:38; the intentions, Heb. 4:12; 1 Pet. 4:1; purpose, Acts 11:23; 2 Cor. 9:7; the will, Rom. 6:17; Col. 3:15; faith, Mark 11:23; Rom. 10:10; Heb. 3:12."[1]

The Greek word for *mind* refers to thinking and understanding; this is a part of the inner person, the seat of which is the heart, that thinks and processes information into understanding, including the making of choices. It is literally "a thinking through, or over, a meditation, reflecting."[2]

> *Jesus replied: "'Love the Lord your God with all your heart and with all your soul and with all your mind.'"*

> Matthew 22:37

We will learn this week that even in terms of our brains, God loves us first and has provided a way for us to love Him in return. He makes His plans known. He gives us warnings. He offers assurance. Always, He promises His love, care, and faithfulness in the midst of our failings. So come with me this week, to discover how our thinking leads us *away* from loving God with all of our minds and what we can do to prevent it.

DAY 1

DEFEAT IS CERTAIN

The Israelites in the desert leave me praying, "Lord, help me not be like *them*!" The people of God repeatedly demonstrated their lack of wholehearted, all-encompassing love for Him. In fact, they were incredulous. Truthfully, they were two-timing, back-stabbing, faithless complainers. The problem is, often I am *exactly* like them.

They saw the glory. They witnessed the miracles and experienced His supernatural provision. They even tasted the fruit in the Promised Land and admitted it was everything He said it would be. But instead of loving Him with all their hearts and minds, they chose a different path, which can traced to a series of lost battles of the mind.

LOST BATTLE #1: DULLED RECEPTION

By the time Moses came on the scene, God's perfect plan of provision had been in motion hundreds of years. Yet the Israelites didn't seem to recognize this reality. They could not recognize the times because they didn't know the promises of God. Let's examine what they could have known.

Read Genesis 15:13–14. What had God told Abraham about his descendants?

_____

_____

_____

Interestingly, when did God bring the people out of captivity (Exodus 12:40–41)?

_____

God is never late in fulfilling His purposes for us. The people should have been ready to hear and expectant of God to act. Instead, we find them losing the next battle of the mind.

LOST BATTLE #2: DISCOURAGEMENT

> *Moses reported this to the Israelites, but they did not listen to him because of their discouragement and cruel bondage.*
>
> Exodus 6:9, NIV 1984

The minds of the enslaved Israelites were essentially closed because of their preoccupation with survival. Even though the news was hope-filled, they could not hear it or take it in. My husband and I understand this mind-set, all too well.

One of our adopted daughters came from a background similar to that of the Israelites enduring cruel bondage in Egypt. We don't know her circumstances from early childhood; however, we can deduce severe neglect based upon her weight and abilities. Her responses to the environment confirm our hunches. Whenever she becomes stressed for any reason, she reverts back to what experts call **survival mode**. Her brain chemistry literally changes. Certain functions are cut off. Only those functions necessary for survival (like securing food and water) and self-preservation remain. No reasoning abilities exist. No emotion is evident. No instructions are received. Everything in her world becomes solely about surviving the moment. It is impossible to talk a person operating within survival mode into a hope-filled place. They physically cannot hear you.

The Israelites had lost all hope of anything changing. Now everything was worse. These slaves were preoccupied with surviving rather than attending to God's hopeful message of deliverance. Like the Israelites, I am most prone to lose heart when I am discouraged. My problems overshadow everything else within view. My spiritual hearing abilities become limited.

Notice that the discouraged Israelites fade into the backdrop until Exodus 12:3. The cruel bondage has not ceased, but there is a change. What do you think brings about this change?

_____

_____

When you are discouraged, what brings about a change in you? How do you find hope?

_____

_____

_____

Maybe you sing. Sometimes I tell my spouse or a trusted Christian friend. I have been known to call my mom. Today my first line of refuge is my Bible. God's Word is always accessible, and I can be vulnerable before the Lord any time of day or night. I tell Him I am discouraged and in great need of a word from Him. He is always faithful to give one, like Numbers 23:19:

> *God is not human, that he should lie, not a human being, that he should change his mind. Does he speak and then not act? Does he promise and not fulfill?*

I wonder how much of the miraculous display of God's rescuing power the Israelites missed during their discouragement. The next audience Moses addressed was Pharaoh, and the "God Show" began. Do you find it interesting that at the peak of the Israelites' discouragement, God was on the eve of working miracles? Don't give up. He just might be on the eve of working wonders in your life too.

LOST BATTLE #3: DISCONTENTMENT

At last, the enslaved Israelites left Egypt, free! Then days into their journey, food became scarce. The whole community grumbled against Moses and Aaron, blaming them for their predicament, and accusing them of trying to kill them by starvation. Scholars agree they were likely out of the food they carried out of Egypt. But was complaining and blaming the leadership the best solution? Read Exodus 16:4–9. In your opinion, what would have been a better way to handle the situation?

_____

_____

_____

Honestly, how many times do we find ourselves grumbling against those God has placed over us? What about those in our jobs, our homes, our families, and our churches? Do we realize the serious nature of our grumblings? What does Moses say about the grumbling behavior in verses 6–7?

_____

_____

What advice does Philippians 2:14 provide regarding complaining?

_____

What if a situation warrants a complaint? The Israelites were out of food. This was serious concern. What does Psalm 64:1 suggest?

_____

"Our extremity is his opportunity."[3]

Paramount in this area of grumbling has been my realization of the end result: I'm helping the enemy! Devoting brain time to grumbling and complaining and then allowing it to flow out of my mouth is tallied a win for the enemy. When I understood the consequences, I made a decision: **not on MY watch!**

I began analyzing where it happens (at home? in the car? when I'm with others?). My personal grumbling occurs when I am alone, during the brief interludes between tasks. Therefore, I'm employing strategies to fight back. In the morning, before the day begins, I pray, "Lord, that kind of destructive thinking cannot come in this place. There is too much at stake. Help me recognize when it enters my thinking. Let it **not** find a resting place in my mind." Also, I'm making efforts to stop thinking those thoughts when I become conscious of them. I turn on some music or move to the next task. Eventually, the grumbling must stop!

What steps can you take to stop grumbling and complaining today?

_____

_____

LOST BATTLE #4: DISTRUST

The complaining and grumbling of the Israelites turned into a judgmental spirit, with constantly pointing fingers at Moses and Aaron. The people no longer asked for what they needed; they demanded it. And if their leaders wouldn't accommodate their demands, they would simply kill them. The people had the audacity to test God by saying, "Is the Lord among us or not?" (Exodus 17:7).

What truly amazes me is not the depravity of man, but the provision of God. Yes, while we are yet sinning, God loves us. Although the Israelites did not deserve it, and they lost the battle of the mind, God caused water to gush out of a rock to meet their need. Our God is patient, and He is kind beyond what we deserve.

Can you think of a time God was generous, kind, and faithful to you in the midst of your own distrust and questioning whether God was with you?

_____

_____

The Israelites' distrust of God's leaders and the very presence of God was a symptom of a greater mental failure on the horizon.

LOST BATTLE #5: DISBELIEF

> *So we see that they were not able to enter [into His rest],*
> *because of their unwillingness to adhere to and trust in and*
> *rely on God [unbelief had shut them out].*
>
> Hebrews 3:19, AMP

The moment of receiving the promise was finally upon God's people, and they blew it. But is it any wonder they failed to believe God after a series of mental losses leading up to this moment for two years? They had trampled on their own believing power. The door stood open, but they were not prepared to walk through it.

Please don't presume this is accidental. God is not the only one who understands the power of the mind to love Him. The enemy awaits the opportune moment to sabotage, steal, and destroy our faith—our very lives (John 10:10). We must be ready. When God sets before us the open door, He fully expects us to walk through it.

> *"Delays are dangerous. They provoke God's spirit. God has set*
> *before you an open door. It will not remain open forever;*
> *it may not remain open long."*[4]

> *See to it, brothers and sisters, that none of you has a*
> *sinful, unbelieving heart that turns away from the living God.*
>
> Hebrews 3:12

If you are staring before an open door, refusing to walk through it because you are struggling with unbelief, start walking. Run, actually. Write today's date and describe the open door you are going through as of now. Then tell your neighbor all about the situation when you come to Bible study.

Today is _____ .

_____

_____

_____

_____

_____

DAY 2

GOOD IS GOOD ENOUGH

For years, my husband wore the same long-sleeved yellow shirt for all major holidays. He loved it because of its quality and soft fabric, but most of all because it felt good. His shirt also packed well and was a perfect fit with a timeless style. What disturbed me was the conspicuous nature of the shirt. Every holiday picture taken during those five years featured Chad's signature yellow pullover. As much as I encouraged him to buy a new favorite, I could not get him to move past this old one. It was comfortable, and he was content wearing it.

What keeps us from loving God with all our minds? The same mind-set that kept Chad in his yellow shirt: our nature for preferring comfort and our contentment with good.

Just before the Israelites crossed over into the Promised Land, one group settled for what they thought was *good* at the expense of the *immeasurable more* God had promised. They settled within their comfort zone but outside God's best plan for them. You and I have the same tendencies. Today we will learn what it takes to reject settling for anything less than God's best by loving Him with all our minds.

REQUIREMENTS FOR LETTING GO OF GOOD

It's time to derail our fast track towards *good*. Unfastening our attachment to comfort, ease and security in the known is a prerequisite to experiencing more than we can ask or imagine (Ephesian 3:20). Let's stop acquiescing to the traveling kiddie rides in the local mall parking lot when we've been given tickets to Disney World. A fanfare of adventure and possibility awaits.

UNDERSTANDING GOD'S CALL UPON OUR LIVES

One thing is clear about the Israelites: they should have known God's promises and call on their lives. It had been passed down from generation to generation from Abraham (Genesis 12:1–7), Isaac (Genesis 26:2–4), Jacob (Genesis 28:12–15), and Joseph (Genesis 50:24–25) to Moses (Exodus 3:7–10).

Yesterday we walked vicariously with the Israelites, who left Egypt yet failed to trust God to deliver them into the Promised Land (Numbers 13). Now the children of those who were taken out of Egypt, those who witnessed the miracles of God and how He took care of them in the desert, enter center stage. Read Numbers 14:31–35. What was God's best plan for their lives?

_____

_____

_____

Is God concerned about the details of our lives? Does He have a best plan for your life and mine? Of course, every person is called to repentance (Acts 17:30). Anyone who calls on His name and believes is called to eternal life (John 3:16). God's will is that we be sanctified (2 Thessalonians 4:3); and that we bring Him glory (Isaiah 43:7). The Bible is instructive in how a believer should live their life from cover to cover.

Does it matter what jobs we select or who we marry? Or whether we marry at all? Do we accept that volunteer position at the food pantry? Should I move to another state? These are questions about which theologians and serious students of the Word disagree. I expect you and I will be no different.

I believe God has a best plan for my life and for every believer integral to our sanctification and development toward holiness. My convictions rest upon the examples found across the writ of Scripture. Throughout the Bible we read accounts of God giving specific tasks to His people. Some examples include Noah (Genesis 6:13); Abraham (Genesis 12:1); Jacob (Genesis 46:3); Moses (Exodus 3:7); Jeremiah (Jeremiah 1:4); Amos (Amos 7:15); Jonah (Jonah 1:1); Philip (Acts 8:26); and Saul (Acts 9:6). We also read of God's plenary involvement in the lives of His people to accomplish His purposes (i.e., Joshua taking Jericho, Joshua 6:2-6; David's battle plans, 2 Samuel 5:23-24; Joseph escaping to Egypt with Jesus, Matthew 2:13; the selection of disciples, Luke 6:12-16; and Paul's movements, Acts 15:6-10). Although our lives may not be prodigious and live on within these holy pages, they are designed to accomplish His specific purposes.

> For we are God's [own] handiwork (His workmanship, created in Christ Jesus, [born anew] that we may do those good works which God predestined (planned beforehand) for us [taking paths which He prepared ahead of time], that we should walk in them [living the good life which He prearranged and made ready for us to live].
>
> Ephesians 2:10, AMP

How important is it for believers in Christ to know God's plan for their lives (Ephesians 5:17)?

_____

_____

_____

Knowing what God desires most for us is a first critical step toward distinguishing **good** from **best**. Maybe you don't know what God has planned for you to be when you grow up. Maybe you are unsure of an exact task given by God specifically for you. That would be something to pray about beginning today. We will look more closely at this subject in week 5. Regardless of where you stand on the issue of God's specific involvement and plan for our lives there are many aspects in life that can be discerned as *good* but not *best*.

We should ask the Lord for direction. Paul instructs us to pray in every circumstance and in everything (Philippians 4:7). For example, we should bring our schedules, responsibilities and hobbies to the feet of Christ. How much time do we spend watching movies or television? Is it too much? How much time do we spend shopping, engaged in sports, tuned into Facebook or our hobbies? I am not talking about keeping up with national news, watching your child's ball games, or getting what your family needs at Wal-Mart. God knows we need to take care of our families and be informed citizens in a lost world. But how much time and energy do we spend on tasks with no eternal significance? What about all that extra time we're so prone to squander? There are areas in each of our lives that we may need to evaluate against God's will for our lives. First of all, if you know God's calling or His will for your life during this season, please write it here.

_____

_____

_____

Next, think of two examples (specific activities or areas that you spend your time on consistently) and fill in the blanks:

Does _____ help accomplish God's will in my life today?

Does _____ contribute to what God has called me to do?

RESISTING THE PATH OF SETTLING FOR WHAT WE THINK IS BEST

Meister Eckhart wrote:

> *"There are plenty to follow our Lord halfway, but not the other half. They will give up possessions, friends, and honors, but it touches them too closely to disown themselves."* [5]

Read Numbers 32:1–5. The Reubenites and Gadites chose to forego the promised best for the known good. Could we share their heart's cry? *"Do not make us cross the Jordan."*

Do we see at least a glimmer of what God has called us to yet cry, "Lord, please let me stay here. Don't make me go in *that* direction. It's good *here*. What's wrong with *here*?" Read the next section in this narrative (vv. 6–15). What is the Moses' opinion of this request by the Reubenites and Gadites? Would you agree or disagree?

_____

_____

_____

Moses speaks as if they have slapped the gift horse in the mouth. Moses already knows he will not have the opportunity to cross the Jordan. Now those privileged to go and experience what he cannot—all the blessing God has promised for generations—do not want to go. The audacity!

The lands in question on the east side of the Jordan were likely more appealing for livestock than the limestone ridges of Palestine. [6] Physically getting their hordes across the Jordan to enter into the Promised Land would also be an obstacle—and don't forget those fortified cities with the Nephilim swarming the territory! The known looked very good indeed.

How do we know we will be successful in what God is asking us to do? How do we know what we are trusting God to give will be better than what we currently enjoy?

> *Now faith is the assurance (the confirmation, the title deed) of the things [we] hope for, being the proof of things [we] do not see and the conviction of their reality [faith perceiving as real fact what is not revealed to the senses].*

> Hebrews 11:1, AMP

When we move from asking these questions and waiting for God to respond and we begin manipulating our situations, just like these tribes, so that we get what we want now, we will always miss the blessing prepared for us.

Notice Numbers 32:16–24. The men persisted in their suitable-land presentation without responding to the accusations of Moses. How did Moses respond to their presentation?

_____

_____

UNDERSTANDING GOD WILL ALLOW US TO SETTLE FOR GOOD AND MISS BEST

Like the Israelite tribes, we tend to settle, and God allows it. He does not force us to cross our Jordans into the promised greatness stored up for us. God may allow good and comfortable to work out, but it would be wrong to assume that simply because the suitable-land presentation works out, it must be God's blessing.

The east side of the Jordan always lies outside of God's promise. The reality for the tribes that settled outside the Promised Land was that they fell into the hands of the Moabites within a short period of time. History records the region as being "a constant battlefield, never attaining a settled prosperity, and . . . conquered before the rest" of the tribes.[7] Perhaps there is benefit to rejecting the comfortable, *known good* to embrace the *unknown best* of God.

RESOLVING TO LEAVE BEHIND THAT WHICH IS IMPORTANT TO US

Jesus had spent enough time in His relationship with His Father to know what to leave behind, and when:

> As the time approached for him to be taken up to heaven, Jesus resolutely set out for Jerusalem.
>
> Luke 9:51

Jesus came to save humanity. Surely He had time to stop for more healing, releasing, and forgiving. Wasn't this what He came to do? Yes. But not *this* way right *now*. A resolute trek to Jerusalem was the only path of obedience.

God has not called us to do everything personally. Frankly, there is always too much work for too few workers. You might be highly gifted and equipped for a particular needed work. You might love doing it. The leaders might not be able to find anyone else as qualified as you. But the question you desperately need to ask is, **"Lord, does this responsibility line up with your purpose and calling for my life right now?"**

I am learning the gravity of sacrificing what I'm called to do (the *best*) in order to accomplish what I'm **not** called to do (the *good*). For example, when I homeschooled my children, my only time to write in a concentrated manner was during the summers while my kids were in camps and activities. Therefore, I did not volunteer at Vacation Bible School. I felt like a slacker, and I looked like a slacker. Volunteering for VBS is a good endeavor. It's what we think dedicated Christian moms do. But for me, choosing the good opportunity expected of me over my writing would have been disobedience. I would have been neglecting *my* calling.

Neither am I helping teach our Sunday school class during the months I'm writing this study. It takes hours to prepare to teach a lesson, which I enjoy. These are good areas of ministry that fit my spiritual gifting. However, the time required to do what is *good* steals time from doing what God has called me to do today. Neither of these *good* ministries lined up with the primary ministry task God has given me at specific times.

For years I attempted too much and made absolutely zero progress on what God had called me to do. Does my church need help in VBS and Sunday school? Yes, but I will need to trust that God can get the job done without my help, in order for me to obedient to Him.

Satan is aware of our callings. His intent is to keep us from obedience. Beth Moore has often said, "If Satan cannot move us to destruction, he will move us to distraction." I was distracted for years.

Is there anything in your life distracting you?

_____

_____

CHOOSING TO EMBRACE THE UNKNOWN CERTAINTY OF GOD'S CALL

This is a deliberate mental choosing. God wants us to look at the absolute impossibility before us and say, *"Lord, this is what I believe you have told me to do to. From the evidence at hand and the measly servant you have to work through, I certify you are absolutely NUTS. But with all I am today, I will believe you. I will follow you into the unseen and unpredictable, because I am convinced you know what's best for me. I will not settle for less than everything you have to give."*

Commit to trust Him this morning, this afternoon, and this evening—today, tomorrow, next week . . . until you get across that mental chasm of unbelief. His unseen *best* is always better than your seen *good*.

DAY 3

KINGS FALTER

Before our family began to swell with children, I was a reading specialist and taught children's literature at the university. I love a great story, masterfully crafted with layers of meaning and multiple connections. So my affection for true stories that include vivid characters, with climax and resolution requiring divine intervention, should be no surprise. The Old Testament is rich with stories God has ordained for us.

> *"Remember that the historical books were almost the only Scripture possessed by the early saints; and from those they learned the mind of God. . . . If rightly viewed, the histories of the Old Testament are full of instruction. They supply us both with warnings and examples in the realm of practical morals; and hidden within their letter, like pearls in oyster shells, lie grand spiritual truths couched in allegory and metaphor."*[8]

Our lesson today catapults us into the midst of a rich story unfolding as Israel becomes a nation led by an anointed king for the first time. God, as King of Israel, has been rejected. Instead, the people clamored to be like everyone else. They asked for an earthly king. In God's omniscience (His all-knowing presence) and His providence, a man is divinely selected. Saul is the right man for the job, yet he ends up losing it to another because of his wrong thinking and poor decision making. It didn't have to end this way. Saul could have been a great king, loving and serving his God with everything he possessed. What went wrong? And what can his life teach us about our own?

SAUL: THE RIGHT CHOICE

Read 1 Samuel 10:1, 9. What two things set Saul apart to prepare him for the kingship?

_____

_____

God did not make a mistake selecting Saul. He equipped Saul in every way. "God turned him around by giving him a changed heart. He grew internally up to the level of his changed circumstances."[9] How does Saul's transformation relate to 2 Corinthians 5:17?

> *Therefore if any person is [ingrafted] in Christ (the Messiah) he is a new creation (a new creature altogether); the old [previous moral and spiritual condition] has passed away. Behold, the fresh and new has come!* (AMP).

_____

_____

God has not made a mistake choosing you either. You are perfect for Him. Your calling is a flawless match to your equipping, complete with a regenerated heart.

THE FALTERINGS OF A RIGHTLY CHOSEN KING

Read 1 Samuel 13:5–14. Shortly into his reign, Saul rallied the troops to fight against the Philistines; however, they were largely ill-equipped for the battle. The Philistines had cornered the market on blacksmiths, and Israel was fighting without swords or spears (1 Samuel 13:19–22). Now the troops were restless and afraid. Some hid in caves. Many had deserted the cause. Saul and his army waited on Samuel, the appointed priest of the Lord, to arrive.

For a moment, turn back to Deuteronomy 20:1–4. What was so important about Samuel being there?

_____

_____

Saul had full knowledge of this requirement. He had waited in this capacity before (1 Samuel 10:8), yet now he refused to wait for Samuel to arrive.

1. Preoccupations

Saul was preoccupied with his new position. He was so busy trying to *keep* his job that he forgot to *do* his job. He should have taken his cues from a riveting story in Exodus where the very forefathers of the people he was now leading found themselves in a similar predicament. The Israelites had been caught between the Egyptian army and the edge of the Red Sea (Exodus 14:9–13). What did Moses do that Saul should have done in his situation?

_____

_____

_____

2. Faulty Assumptions

It's also very possible that Saul intended to shake things up a bit with the dawning of a new political day. If he could dispense with the need for Samuel, in front of the people, it would mean the kingship possessed the power to invent other ways than those established by God for meeting pressing dangers.[10] In other words, Israel could **FINALLY** be like every other nation, relying on the monarchy for leadership and direction, with only a token nod to religion.

3. Shaken, Not Stirred

Saul's circumstances were scary and uncertain. His new world was crumbling around him. Saul allowed his surroundings to *shake* his trust in God rather than *stir* him toward greater faith in God's ability to deal with the situation. Saul made the decision to *act* when he had been told to *wait*.

I am familiar with his misstep. I have decided I could handle a situation better alone. I know the mental distress of sensing your surroundings are crumbling and will fall to pieces if something isn't done immediately! I have experienced the sinfulness of feeling shaken and acting when God has clearly told me to wait. What about you?

_____

_____

_____

4. Justifiable Excuses

Saul's explanation to Samuel is very telling:

> Saul replied, "When I saw that the men were scattering, and that you did not come at the set time, and that the Philistines were assembling at Micmash, I thought, 'Now the Philistines will come down against me at Gilgal, and I have not sought the LORD's favor.' So I felt compelled to offer the burnt offering."
>
> 1 Samuel 13:11–12

I see some red flags in this explanation, don't you? Underline places in Saul's justification for his actions that might communicate there was a problem with how he made decisions.

Re-read Deuteronomy 20:1–3 and circle what Saul *should* have done in response to the frightful circumstances:

> When you go to war against your enemies and see horses and chariots and an army greater than yours, do not be afraid of them, because the LORD your God, who brought you up out of Egypt, will be with you. When you are about to go into battle, the priest shall come forward and address the army. He shall say: . . . "Do not be fainthearted or afraid; do not panic or be terrified by them."

5. Deceptive Reasoning

James 1:22–25 warns us that our reasoning abilities lead us away from doing what we know God has instructed us to do. How might these verses apply to your love relationship with the Lord?

_____

_____

_____

Sometimes God asks us to do things that seem irrational. Let's be honest: periodically what we think God is saying to us seems a little whacky! When people learned we were adopting a sibling group of four, on top of the four children we already had, not everyone thought that was a brilliant idea:

"You are going to do what?"

"Don't you already have four children?"

"Do you realize what your family picture is going to look like?"

"Is your house big enough for ten people?"

"What are you going to drive?"

These were all reasonable questions. In fact, I found myself waking up during the night in a cold sweat, realizing new reasons our plan was a crazy idea. Realities like these hit me:

I do not have enough forks (thirty) for one whole day!

Eight kids—Wow! That's expensive—how in the world are we going to pay for this?

They can't speak English.

How am I going to do their hair?

The most unsettling deception in my mind came as a question about how I would ever fulfill God's calling to write and speak if we took on this enormous, life-draining task. We had plenty of wise and prudent reasons to walk away, except one: this was what God had told us to do. Herein lies Saul's downfall . . . *"So I felt compelled."*

Likely you too have a list of good and sound reasons for faltering in loving God with all your mind. What are some deceptive thoughts that have led you away from obedience in the past?

_____

_____

_____

Sometimes I've failed. Other times, for which I'm thankful, as in this last adoption, my love for God has overcome my destructive thinking. What about you? Have you had successes? Share one below.

_____

_____

_____

_____

Essentially, we must understand the clear call of God upon Saul's life. God set Saul in the kingship for **success**, not for failure. God does the same for us. When He sets us apart for a task, role, or a particular lot in life, He does so with the intent and desire that we will be successful in that role or task. He does not play Gotcha! with us. His desire is to see you and me blossom and live lives of fruitfulness. Taking our cues and inspiration from the lessons God gives us through His stories will help us as we grow to love Him more each day.

DAY 4

SUCCESSES ARE TROUNCED

Last week, we studied a king noted for his wholehearted pursuit of God: King Asa, who came to the throne and cleaned house. He crushed much of the sanctioned badness the people of God had practiced for generations. When crisis came, he ran to God, and God brought the victory. Asa met his hindrance-defeating moments and won.

Like you and me, Asa had more than one opportunity to choose God over everything else. Read 2 Chronicles 16:1–6. What did Asa choose to do in the face of this military crisis?

_____

_____

Most scholars believe Baasha, king of Israel, to have been a much smaller threat than the hordes Asa faced against Zerah. Asa likely thought it was a local problem he could handle like all other kings. Asking rulers to break their alliances, as he did with the Syrians, was common practice, although morally wrong. It also appeared to be a smart political move, which it did turn out to be.

WRONG THINKING BREEDS WRONG BEHAVIOR

We too try to handle what we consider smaller, or local, matters without relying on God as we would in a crisis situation. Interestingly, a common phenomenon is found among Christ followers: "Believers frequently behave worse in little trials than in the great ones."[11] When was the last time you decided you could handle a problem yourself instead of taking it to the Lord? How did that work out for you?

_____

_____

_____

_____

You and I also tend to align our circumstances to cultural norms, regardless of adherence to truth. If our situation "works out," too often we see it as divine providence—God's approval. Charles H. Spurgeon warned that there are providences of Satan as well as of God.[12] When something works out, we should not assume that is a God-ordained green light. It could very much be the result of enemy activity attempting to lead us astray. For certain, "A wrong is a wrong, whatever comes of it."[13] It does not get past God unnoticed.

WRONG THINKING BRINGS PENALTIES

Fortunately, God places people in our lives to encourage as well as chastise us when the moment is right. Read 2 Chronicles 16:7–9. Here we are shown God eagerly awaiting opportunities to help those who are "blameless" or "completely dedicated to him."[14] What do these verses communicate about individuals who choose NOT to be completely dedicated to God?

_____

If you continue reading (vv. 10–14), the situation moves from bad to worse. Whatever lessons Asa learned in his first fifteen years of leading Judah and seeking God wholeheartedly, he lost in the last twenty-five. Whatever happened during those later years, we will not know. There are no records of wars, difficulties, or struggles. We can assume everything went well for Asa and that life was relatively uneventful. It's the sort of environment that breads complacency. Unfortunately, complacency destroys tenacity.

I will not begin to pretend to understand the complacent mind-set. I have eight children, ages five to fourteen. I rarely sit down, unless I'm writing. I even eat standing up some days. Crazy as it may seem, there is simply no room for complacency in my life today. However, I recognize the danger that looms in front of me when life responsibilities may decrease over the years. Maybe your life pace has slowed from what it once was. Now what? How do you keep your tenacity for pursuing God completely and for rejecting complacency?

RIGHT THINKING ENCOURAGED

One suggestion I see lived out in front of me is the mental rejection of retirement in Christian living. I am not suggesting we keep the same pace we had twenty years ago, going as hard or as fast or as long as we once did. However, we'd better still be going and striving to become who God has purposed us to become. Idleness can be problematic at any age. It was for David (when he sinned with Bathsheba), Solomon (his entire reign), and Asa, who had just come out of a long span of peacetime in Judah. Such idleness may be the thing that needs to go in your life. D. L. Moody once said:

> "It is observable that God has often called men to places of dig-
> nity and honor when they have busy and honest employment....
> Saul was seeking his father's donkeys and David his father's
> sheep when called to the Kingdom. The shepherds were feeding
> their flocks when they had their glorious revelation.
> God called the four apostles from their fishing and Matthew
> from collecting taxes, Amos from the horsemen of Tecoah,
> Moses from keeping Jethro's sheep, Gideon from the threshing
> floor, Elisha from the plows. God never called a lazy man.
> God never encourages idleness and will not despise persons in
> the lowest employment."[15]

There are two women in my church who clearly qualify for the senior's discount at restaurants and shops and likely have for a decade. Abbie leads our young mom's share group each week, mentors various others she latches on to, and does a host of other things in the community. The other precious lady is in that same camp. Margey is dearly loved by my Sunday school class of over seventy-five nearly and newly marrieds. She and her husband, Jim, are retired missionaries who continue to serve all ages. There are often people staying in their home, such as the three families who were recently evacuated from an emergency in our area. Such chaos is a normal state in Margey's life of service to others. In fact, she is bringing my family dinner this evening to enable me to keep writing. And there are more women in my church of whom I could speak. They are actively living out 1 Corinthians 15:58:

> *Always give yourselves fully to the work of the Lord, because*
> *you know that your labor in the Lord is not in vain.*

Here is what you need to hear: WE NEED YOU. You are needed exactly where *you* are in *your* walk of life, with *your* gifts. If you are a young woman, God has something unique for this period of your life. If you are busy with raising a family, the Lord has not exempted you from bearing spiritual fruit within and outside of your family. If your children are grown and you have more time than you have ever needed in your life—do not think this is an accident. Regardless of our ages, God is not finished with us until we quit breathing:

> *He who began a good work in you will carry it on to completion*
> *until the day of Christ Jesus.*
>
> Philippians 1:6

Pray about what God would have you do right where you are. Make yourself available to Him today. We would all love to share in the blessing of you!

Thank you, Lord, that you never let us go—that you continue to grow us, improve us, and use us until you take us home. I pray that you will provide people in our lives to help us and encourage us to follow you with reckless abandon. And as we progress in this life, I ask that you keep our eyes on you—whether we are in a busy stage of life or one more peaceful. Always keep us mindful of how to follow you wherever we are. In the sweet name of Jesus, amen.

DAY 5

SMALL THINKING REIGNS

Along this journey of seeking what it looks like to love God with my entire mind, there is one lesson I need continuously drilled into my hard head. As you read through the next pages that conclude our study of thinking gone awry, please know that both the subject and the pointed presentation are directed at myself before anyone else. I need it this way. I wonder if you need it this way too.

Stop thinking so small! Stop talking yourself out of believing that God can accomplish the miraculous using your life. *Take back the promises* and methods of God you have rejected because you thought they couldn't possibly be meant for you. Take them back by letting go!

God does not call us to small thinking. Small thinking results from a lack of exposure *to* the Word and a lack of ownership of the Word. Today, let the Word of God speak possibility and limitlessness over you. Maybe you have never given God the opportunity to dream with your life. Maybe you are afraid to take that next step for fear you will be disappointed. Maybe you feel insignificant, convinced *small* is just your size. *Leave it behind.* Small thinking limits who we become and what we are able to accomplish in the Lord.

The enemy knows this. He is constantly filling our minds with thoughts and ideas contrary to the Word, and even though they are opposed to the Word of God, these thoughts can make sense to me. They confine possibilities to what I can see. They confirm my own beliefs about my weaknesses. They keep me from loving the Lord with all my mind and restrain me from taking that next step of faith.

Sweet friend, it's time for you and me to let go of small thinking. God calls His people to tasks and opportunities greater than we can imagine. Look at the following examples found across the whole writ of Scripture. Let them rest on you. Ponder the possible ramifications these examples have on your outlook of what God might have in store for you.

OLD TESTAMENT EXAMPLES

Read the passages and record anything that demonstrates God calling us to enlarge our thinking.

Genesis 18:14

> *Is anything too hard for the LORD?*

_____

_____

Genesis 22:15–18

_____

_____

Joshua 1:1–5

_____

_____

Judges 4:4–7

_____

_____

Esther 2:17–18; 4:14

> *Now the king was attracted to Esther more than to any of the other women, and she won his favor. . . . So he set a royal crown on her head and made her queen. . . . "And who knows but that you have come to your royal position for such a time as this?"*

_____

_____

Jeremiah 1:4–10

_____

_____

Amos 7:14–15

> Amos answered Amaziah, "I was neither a prophet nor the son
> of a prophet, but I was a shepherd, and I also took care of syca-
> more-fig trees. But the LORD took me from tending the flock and
> said to me, 'Go, prophesy to my people Israel.' "

_____

_____

How do these examples influence your understanding of the thinking God calls us to embrace?

_____

_____

NEW TESTAMENT EXAMPLES

Never does God encourage mediocrity or call His people to easy and comfortable. On the contrary, God demonstrates much higher intentions. Paul described God this way:

> The God who gives life to the dead and calls things that are not
> as though they were.

> Romans 4:17, NIV 1984

Like Father, like Son. How do the following words of Jesus demonstrate He is a chip off the ol' Block when it comes to stretching us to think bigger?

Matthew 14:15–16

_____

_____

Matthew 17:20

> "Truly I tell you, if you have faith as small as a mustard seed,
> you can say to this mountain, 'Move from here to there,' and it
> will move. Nothing will be impossible for you."

_____

_____

Matthew 19:26

> Jesus looked at them and said, "With man this is impossible,
> but with God all things are possible."

_____

Matthew 21:22

If you believe, you will receive whatever you ask for in prayer.

Mark 9:22–23

"But if you can do anything, take pity on us and help us."
"'If you can'?" said Jesus.
"Everything is possible for one who believes."

Luke 5:4–11

Luke 11:9–13

We could go on and on. Suffice it to say, letting go of small thinking is God's idea. In order to love God with all our minds, we must let go of small thinking.

LET'S BEGIN TODAY

In light of His promises and dealings with those He loves, ask the Lord what He would have you do.

There is work to be done. Someone with just *your* personality, with *your* gifting, in *your* situation is exactly who God needs to accomplish His will (Ephesians 2:10). Anything He asks you to do is important, purposeful, and significant.

When you get a word you believe is to you, write it down. Tell someone. Ask Him to confirm it. Meanwhile, keep seeking to make sure it is, indeed, what He is instructing you to do. Because like Peter's experience walking on water, what He is asking you to do will most likely not be small—but impossible, unachievable, and way out of your league:

Who despises the day of small things?

Zechariah 4:10, NIV 1984

That question is equivalent to asking, "*Can anyone, after these promises and prophecies, presume to be doubtful about the future?*"[16]

In spite of the difficulties and impossibilities ahead . . . get to work.

In the words of Henry Blackaby:

> "*After many years of walking with God and seeking to go deeper with Him, I've drawn this conclusion: We limit God. We determine much of what we experience of God's power. And we set parameters on the depth of our relationship with God. In spite of limitless possibilities, we choose to impede what God does in our lives, so that He must say to us, 'I spoke to you, rising up early and speaking, but you did not hear, and I called you, but you did not answer' (Jeremiah 7:13).*"[17]

> *So also Abraham "believed God, and it was credited to him as righteousness."*

> Galatians 3:6

The term "credited" Paul uses means to "reckon, count, compute" and is associated with accounting.[18] What if God is counting, or keeping a record—not of our sins, but of the times we choose Him over everything else? He is calling us to act out of minds willing to believe bigger thoughts and greater possibilities. When we choose to reject small thinking and embrace the difficult—even the impossible—to labor and love for His name's sake (Hebrews 6:10), He does not let it slip past Him.

On the day when I stand before the Lord and everything I have thought or done is no longer hidden, (Revelation 20:12) it will not be my finest hour. I will be ashamed, filled with regret and remorse. But I will be rescued by the blood of the Lamb. Because of Jesus, I will stand blameless before God. *It's the missed opportunities that I fear.*

What if God were to show us what **could have been** if we would have only let Him do what He dreamed for our lives? What would my life have been like if I would have loved Him with my mind enough to set Him free to do what only He could accomplish in a life like mine? If there is eternal blessing to be had from a life spent allowing God to do whatever could be done in my measly life and yours—let us ask Him to bring it on:

> *Now to Him Who, by (in consequence of) the [action of His] power that is at work within us, is able to [carry out His purpose and] do superabundantly, far over and above all that we [dare] ask or think [infinitely beyond our highest prayers, desires, thought, hopes, or dreams]—To Him be glory in the church and in Christ Jesus throughout all generations forever and ever. Amen (so be it).*

> Ephesians 3:20–21, AMP

ENDNOTES

1. W. E. Vine. *Vine's Expository Dictionary of Old and New Testament Words*, (Iowa: World Bible, 1981), 205.

2. Ibid., 69

3. J. Orr, *The Pulpit Commentary*, H. D. M. Spence, Joseph S. Exell, eds., (Grand Rapids: Wm. B. Eerdmans, 1958), 1:32.

4. W. Binnie, *The Pulpit Commentary*, 2:164.

5. Meister Eckhart, *Meister Eckhart: The Essential Writings* (New York: HarperOne, 2009), 389.

6. Winterbotham, *The Pulpit Commentary*, 2:417.

7. Ibid.

8. Charles H. Spurgeon, *Sermons of Rev. C. H. Spurgeon of London* (New York: Funk & Wagnalls, 1900), 10:68.

9. R. Payne Smith, *The Pulpit Commentary*, H. D. M. Spence, Joseph S. Exell, eds., (Grand Rapids: Wm. B. Eerdmans, 1962), 4:176.

10. C. Chapman, *The Pulpit Commentary*, H. D. M. Spence, Joseph S. Exell, eds., (Grand Rapids: Wm. B. Eerdmans, 1962), 4:232.

11. Spurgeon, *Sermons*, 10:73.

12. Ibid., 78.

13. Ibid., 79.

14. Traylor, *Layman's Bible Book Commentary*, 124.

15. Robert J. Morgan, *Nelson's Complete Book of Stories, Illustrations, and Quotes*, (Nashville: Thomas Nelson, 2000), 800.

16. W. J. Deane, *The Pulpit Commentary*, H. D. M. Spence, Joseph S. Exell, eds., (Grand Rapids: Wm. B. Eerdmans, 1963), 14:41.

17. Richard Blackaby, *Unlimiting God*, (Colorado Springs: Multnomah, 2008), 16.

18. BibleHub.com. Thayer's Greek Lexicon, Electronic Database, 2011, by Biblesoft Inc. (accessed October 30, 2014). http://biblehub.com/greek/3049.htm

NOTES

LESSON 5

WHEN THOUGHTS OVERCOME

Welcome to the halfway mark for learning how to respond to God's love with everything we are. If you are thinking, I am way over my head here, you are absolutely correct. Consider yourself engulfed, swallowed up, immersed, inundated by Love. The King's love infuses you— from the bottoms of your feet to the royal hair upon your head.

His love has healed every bruise and erased all your blemishes.

His love has triumphed over all your inadequacies.

His love has saturated your empty places.

It is incessant, perpetual, and personal.

You are one He longs to spend today with.

But do you believe it?

Are you receiving God's love as an unchanging reality? Does it impact the way you hold up your head? Does it bring confidence to your personality? Does His love for you increase the volume of your voice while worshiping in the car? Does He make you dance when no one else can see?

My guess would be no. Well, maybe sometimes. But generally, you and I are too lost in our own ineffective thought lives. We succumb to believing, instead, our powerlessness and unfitness for His love. Some of us are so immersed in our own families and social circles that His love never crosses our minds. Some, in our own ways, simply renounce it due to our unworthiness and incompetency. "No! He couldn't possibly love me." Round and round we go, remaining, as it were, on the mental merry-go-round of marginalism.

It's time to get off this ride and cease going back to it.

We *CAN* triumph over typical mental derailments, mediocre musings, and our tendencies to think too small. Advancing to the next spiritual step can become our reality, and we can have assurance of making the right decisions in our lives. We must not forget that God has supernaturally equipped each one of us with the capacity to love Him completely. If Jesus specifically calls us to love Him with all our minds, He fully intends for the Holy Spirit to equip us and the Bible to instruct us.

What does it look like to love Him completely with our minds? Must we hang around the library buried in exegeses and hermeneutics? Do we need to drop everything on the calendar to pray without ceasing—*literally*? Should each of us enroll in seminary and dedicate our lives to full-time Christian ministry? Or should I simply drive around in my car, listening to a constant stream of dramatized audio Bible interspersed with praise and worship music to drown out my carnal thinking? Should I buy a fish to stick on my car and Christian ringtones for my phone? Well, no, not exactly. **But we should think differently.**

DAY 1

WE KNOW HIM INTIMATELY

Isn't it just like God to take something I thought was going to be a weighty responsibility and make it lighter—with the monkey completely on *His* back? (I don't know if you have noticed, but that seems to be His style.) As a believer, I have been given a new heart (2 Corinthians 5:17). This renovated heart is what allows me to love Him because He first loved me. This impossibility-made-possible through the death and resurrection of Christ and the gift of the Holy Spirit has been our focus for the first weeks of our study. However, have you realized that in this supernatural transformation, you and I are also equipped with the *very mind of Christ*?

> "Who has known the mind of the Lord so as to instruct him?"
> But we have the mind of Christ.
>
> 1 Corinthians 2:16

Our ability to *literally* think differently is granted through the Holy Spirit. Can you grasp the magnitude of these two truths? You and I have been given the supernatural capacity to think *beyond* our IQs, to become *more* insightful, *more* resourceful, *more* analytical, *deeper* thinking, *wisdom-richer* women of God. It can happen to you and to me, but it does not happen instantly. According to Romans 12:2, how does it happen?

_____

_____

We might think of *conform* as meaning how something adheres to a mold or pattern.[1] Paul communicates that we are to be finished with our old pattern of thinking. Instead, our thinking is to be *"transformed."* The Greek word for *transformed, metamorphoō,* means "to be transfigured or changed in form." What English word comes to mind?

_____

Paul says, in essence, "Get off the merry-go-round that keeps you spinning in ineffective and destructive thoughts. You don't have to ride it!" The reality of complete and total change in our thinking can be ours. We have been given the mind of Christ. At the same time, we have personal responsibility to stop conforming and to work to renew our minds. This juncture is where the metamorphosis occurs.

Taking full advantage of what we've been given, we should develop habits of thinking that foster lives that love God completely and bid farewell to the mental ride to nowhere. The first transformation occurs though our understanding and acceptance of His love toward us, which expands and intensifies as we get to know Him.

In the words of Charles Spurgeon:

> "Oh, chew the cud of this blessed thought; roll it under your
> tongue as a dainty morsel; sit down this afternoon,
> if you have leisure, and think of nothing but this—his great
> love wherewith he loves you;"[2]

> "When we believe, know, and feel that God loves us, we,
> as a natural result, love him in return; and in proportion as our
> knowledge increases, our faith strengthens, and our
> conviction deepens that we are really beloved of God; we . . .
> are constrained to yield our hearts to God in return."[3]

God desires for you and me to know Him with increasing intimacy and by personal experience, because this is precisely how our love for Him grows. How does Jeremiah 9:23–24 communicate God's yearning to be known by His children?

_____

HE WANTS US TO KNOW HIM

John Piper has said:

> "Therefore, God has given us minds so that,
> by thinking with the Spirit's help, we can know the truth and
> beauty and worth of God through Jesus and treasure him above
> all things and spend our lives expressing this in as many ways
> as our minds can pursue."[4]

The value of knowing God personally can be recognized from the testimonies and life experiences of remarkable characters throughout the Bible. Read the following verses. How did their copious experience with God emanate from the relationship they shared?

Exodus 33:11

_____

_____

2 Samuel 7:18–21

_____

_____

1 Kings 19:9–11

_____

_____

John 7:29; 10:14–15

_____

_____

Our English word *know* is more than a single verb in the Greek. In John 7:29, the Greek verb for *know* refers to an intimate or a full, intimate and complete of knowledge of the Father. The Greek verb *"know"* in John 10:14–15 expresses a constant and progressive growth in experiential knowledge.[5] Although the word uses are different, we can draw the conclusion that Jesus is communicating a rich, layered, and personal knowledge of God. This knowing goes far beyond recall of facts to lived and breathed communion.

The Holy Spirit dwelt in Jesus from conception (Matthew 1:20). You and I receive the same Holy Spirit when we accept Jesus as Lord and Savior of our lives. Philippians 2:6–7 tells us that although Jesus remained complete deity, He set His equality with God aside by choice and humbled himself to come to earth wholly human. For us, what that means is that *we* can know God through the same channels that Jesus, as a man on this planet, knew God. Everything Jesus possessed to know the Father as a human being is accessible to each of us.

HOW DO WE KNOW GOD?

Read the following verses and record what you discover about how to know God:

Proverbs 2:3–61

> *If you call out for insight and cry aloud for understanding, and if you look for it as for silver and search for it as for hidden treasure, then you will understand the fear of the LORD and find the knowledge of God. For the LORD gives wisdom, and from his mouth come knowledge and understanding.*

_____

_____

1 Chronicles 28:9

> *And you, my son Solomon, acknowledge the God of your father, and serve him with wholehearted devotion and with a willing mind, for the LORD searches every heart and understands every desire and every thought. If you seek him, he will be found by you; but if you forsake him, he will reject you forever.*

Acts 17:11

_____

_____

WHAT SHOULD WE KNOW?

What kinds of things should we strive to know about God? The following verses should give us an idea. This is just a minor sampling to whet your appetite. Jot down key words or phrases as you conduct your search.

1. His Personality

Genesis 16:13

_____

_____

Exodus 34:6-7

> And he passed in front of Moses, proclaiming, "The Lord, the
> Lord, the compassionate and gracious God, slow to anger,
> abounding in love and faithfulness, maintaining love to thou-
> sands, and forgiving wickedness, rebellion and sin. Yet he does
> not leave the guilty unpunished."

_____

_____

2. His Expectations

Matthew 6:33

_____

_____

Matthew 22:29

> Jesus replied, "You are in error because you do not know the
> Scriptures or the power of God."

_____

_____

Mark 12:28-31

_____

_____

3. His Love

Luke 19:10

_____

_____

Ephesians 3:17-20

> And I pray that you, being rooted and established in love, may
> have power, together with all the Lord's holy people, to grasp
> how wide and long and high and deep is the love of Christ, and
> to know this love that surpasses knowledge—that you may be
> filled to the measure of all the fullness of God.

_____

_____

Possessing knowledge about God is so very important. It's essential. But there is *more* to knowing Him that leads us into the experiential knowledge Jesus had in mind:

> *Therefore, holy brothers and sisters, who share in the heavenly calling, fix your thoughts on Jesus, whom we acknowledge as our apostle and high priest.*

Hebrews 3:1

The Greek verb for *fix* means "to pay attention, notice, observe; consider, contemplate." It has a strong implication that the attention paid is intense, and the contemplation is broad and thorough, resulting in complete understanding.[6]

Look closely at the following verses and record different ways we can *"fix [our] thoughts on Jesus"*:

Daniel 8:5

> *As I was thinking about this, . . .*

_____

_____

Psalm 119:15

> *I will meditate on Your precepts and have respect to Your ways [the paths of life marked out by Your law]* (AMP).

_____

_____

Acts 10:19

_____

_____

 WORD STUDY

Here, in Acts 10:19, the word thought comes from a Greek verb of great "motion" of thought. Peter was revolving in his mind, in and out, to find the meaning of the visions.[7]

WHY DO SOME PEOPLE KNOW GOD MORE INTIMATELY?

Why do some people seem to know so much more of God? Some people read their Bibles and come away with an exciting word from God regularly, and some don't. Some people seem to have an uncanny connection between God hearing their prayers and receiving answers. Why?

I can answer this question in two words: **spiritual maturity.** Spiritual maturity is not limited to age or the number of years spent as a Christian. Like any relationship, growth and intimacy require time coupled with focused attention.

I spoke with a retired pastor whose wife had recently passed away after forty years of marriage. I inquired about their life together in the early days and learned she had been ten years younger than he. As he mentioned the age difference, he confessed, "You know, I was not very mature. I really needed ten more years to grow up before meeting her."

I too am a late bloomer in some aspects of my relationship with God. Early in my teen years, I had already learned to distinguish the voice of the Holy Spirit from other competing influences and voices. However, if God asked me to do something beyond what I could imagine for myself, I hesitated to believe Him. The mountains were too steep and immovable. Honestly, if I knew God then like I know Him today (experientially as well as with a deeper understanding of His Word), those impossibilities that kept me from believing God—those mountains that wouldn't move—might have been crushed. But I did not have the capacity to know Him in the ways we have investigated today, so I did not mature quickly. As John Piper has said, "Our human minds can only handle so much. Our spiritual maturity limits us. If we have a shallow walk with God, we cannot expect to receive deep revelations from Him. God will match His words to us with our capacity to receive them."[8]

There are no shortcuts to knowing God. It's a process that takes time. But we *can* cooperate, leaving the shallow offerings of religion behind to pick up the pace of maturation. Today, think about what you can do to step up your process of knowing Him. Do you need to spend more time with Him? Do you need to know more about Him? Can you make yourself more available for Him to speak to you? Are there parts of the Word you know it's time to memorize? Is there any way you can clear your schedule for a lunch hour, one of your child's nap times, an afternoon, or a whole day—to listen, think, ponder, pray, and take God's Word into your mind? What ideas are coming to mind right now?

_____

_____

_____

_____

_____

_____

_____

Knowing God experientially like Jesus did, combined with a thorough knowledge of His Word, is the path to learning to love God with all our minds. John Piper reminds us that to " 'love God with all your mind' means engaging all your powers of thought to know God as fully as possible in order to treasure him for all he is worth."[9]

Paul proclaims exactly this in Philippians 3:10:

> I want to know Christ—yes, to know the power of his
> resurrection and participation in his sufferings.

This is what we are to aim toward. Spiritual maturation, here we come. We are walking away from the mental merry-go-round.

DAY 2

WE THINK MORE PROFOUNDLY

The first study I wrote focused on theology and apologetics but was similar in style to this one. Every publishing house with whom I interviewed (except this one) gave the same response: "This book is on a completely different level than most women think, and they won't buy it." That was somewhat hard to believe. What was more disheartening was the possibility they were *right*. After a perusal of shelves at my local bookstores, these experts seemed to be on to an unsettling trend.

You and I buy books about things we feel we need to do, for instance (and I'm generalizing), how to get organized, handle stress, lose weight, and become an awesome Christian mom in only five minutes a day. We don't buy books beckoning us to deeper places with God, such as *Ruthless Trust* (by Brennan Manning), *Think!* (by John Piper), *Slave* (by John MacArthur), and *Fearless* (Max Lucado). I decided the problem was with me and put the study in a drawer. Outside of those of you bold enough to purchase *this* Bible study and complete half of it so far, the marketplace seems to have an accurate pulse on how women generally think, *or so I assumed.*

What if, as a culture, women have found harmless options, such as Pinterest, Facebook, reality TV, and the lighter things of God *more palatable* than the hard work of total transformation? What if we (the general market of Christian women) have simply "conformed to a mold or pattern" of simplemindedness and surface Christianity? Suppose the power given us through the Holy Spirit to engage our minds in kingdom purposes has been largely untapped? Could it be the problem with not seeking the deeper theological quest lies with our conformity to a mold of complacency rather than an eager desire for knowledge?

TO THINK OR NOT TO THINK

We have been given the mind of Christ for the purpose of using it to love God more completely. It's time we reject the light-thinking and time-squandering patterns of this world. Instead, may we be transfigured into the Christ-minded, deeper-thinking versions of ourselves.

Why am I convinced God wants us to be thinkers? Read these verses and jot down anything that might lead you to the answer:

Proverbs 15:14

_____

_____

Jeremiah 29:13

_____

_____

Matthew 6:33

_____

_____

Hebrews 11:6

_____

_____

Although the words for *seek* vary in Hebrew as well as Greek, they carry similar meanings of searching, inquiring about, investigating, desiring to possess, striving for, even seeking earnestly.[10]

Psalm 63:6

_____

_____

Psalm 64:9

_____

_____

Proverbs 14:8

> _The wisdom of the prudent is to give thought to their ways._

_____

_____

Jeremiah 33:3

_____

_____

Ephesians 5:17

> _Therefore do not be foolish, but understand what the_
> _Lord's will is._

_____

_____

TAKE TIME TO EXERCISE YOUR MIND

The current age, even marginal Christianity, accepts and expects vague, thoughtless, and foolish thinking. Just take a quick glance at what people purchase, devote family time to pursue, and talk about over lunch. A woman endowed with the mind of Christ should reject foolish thinking altogether but also refuse to settle for thoughtless or vague. Such thinking is not becoming; neither does it exemplify Christ living in us. We should exercise our minds in the following ways. As you read each verse, take some time to think about how you can begin putting the words into practice. Write down your thoughts or ideas as the Holy Spirit leads you.

> _from Issachar, men who understood the times and knew what_
> _Israel should do. . . ._
>
> 1 Chronicles 12:32

_____

_____

And set your minds and keep them set on what is above (the higher things), not on the things that are on the earth

Colossians 3:2, AMP

_____

_____

But refuse and avoid irreverent legends (profane and impure and godless fictions, mere grandmothers' tales) and silly myths, and express your disapproval of them. Train yourself toward godliness (piety), [keeping yourself spiritually fit].

1 Timothy 4:7, AMP

_____

_____

Therefore, prepare your minds for action; be self-controlled; set your hope fully on the grace to be given you when Jesus Christ is revealed.

1 Peter 1:13, NIV 1984

_____

_____

For the rest, brethren, whatever is true, whatever is worthy of reverence and is honorable and seemly, whatever is just, whatever is pure, whatever is lovely and lovable, whatever is kind and winsome and gracious, if there is any virtue and excellence, if there is anything worthy of praise, think on and weigh and take account of these things [fix your minds on them].

Philippians 4:8, AMP

_____

_____

QUESTIONS TO PONDER

Spend some time thinking about your thinking today (something known as metacognition). Read over the verses from our lesson. Let them permeate your brain over the next week. Google some background information about them. Then think about the following questions:

Do I believe I can actually transform my thinking and operate my days utilizing the mind of Christ?

If so, how can I practice putting on the mind of Christ?

What kinds of resources do I utilize to grow in my faith? Are they pushing me to be transformed? Or are they allowing me to remain comfortable with a happy thought?

What is one major change I need to make regarding my current thought patterns?

Come back to this page after you have done some thinking and write down your thoughts and ideas for getting started.

_____

_____

_____

_____

_____

_____

_____

_____

_____

The mind is where today's war is being waged, and unfortunately, much of the church is losing ground in the midst of current culture. We are curious about many things, always taking in information from various venues. Could it be we simply are not interested in accessing the mind of Christ?

The forwarding of the gospel and the deepening of the church requires thinkers who set their minds on the things of God, who train themselves to be godly, and who diligently prepare their minds for whatever God might bring their way. Won't you take a first step toward total transformation? **Just think.**

DAY 3

WE RELINQUISH AND TRUST

I first saw *The Passion of Christ*, produced by Mel Gibson, on Easter in a small West Texas theater. The most memorable and moving scene came as Jesus was in His horrifying state: beaten until unrecognizable, exhausted, and about to endure the sin of all of humanity and the turning away of His Father. The cross is lying on the ground. Jesus crawls of His own free will upon that cursed structure and stretches out His arms for them to kill Him.

No other visual compares with this one as I think of John 10:17–18, where Jesus says:

> *The reason my Father loves me is that I lay down my life—only to take it up again. No one takes it from me, but I lay it down of my own accord. I have authority to lay it down and authority to take it up again. This command I received from my Father.*

I wonder if these words and the actions of Jesus that followed them influenced Paul's concept of living sacrifice:

> *Therefore, I urge you, brothers and sisters, in view of God's mercy, to offer your bodies as a living sacrifice, holy and pleasing to God—this is your true and proper worship.*
>
> Romans 12:1

Have you ever considered what part of us controls whether we heave ourselves upon that altar in the first place? And which part pulls us off? In the space provided, write out the verse that follows Romans 12:1. It should be familiar to you at this stage in the week, and will provide a clue to the answer to our question.

Romans 12:2

_____

_____

_____

I don't have a definitive answer, but I know myself and my girlfriends. What controls my decision to heave or hold is the same part of me that chooses cheese balls over apple slices. It's the same part of me that replays the tape of hateful scenarios of what I *should* have said to that awful woman instead of practicing pure thinking, thankfulness, or anything praiseworthy. Just as we operate the renewing function with our thoughts, we decide in our own minds to what degree, when, and how we offer ourselves as living sacrifices before the Lord. I have the power, using nothing but my mental faculties, to lay my life down on that imaginary altar and to pick it up again. And so do you.

Today we are looking closely at this relationship between the concept of laying our lives down and taking them up again in the form of relinquishing and trusting. This is a relationship wrought with tension. We can envision this relationship in the lives of biblical examples. In fact, we will almost be able to feel the tension, because we all know what it's like to struggle with everything in us to resist doing what we *want*, in the hope of experiencing a superior outcome. How we handle this tension in our daily walk will determine the degree to which we love God with our entire minds.

EXAMPLE #1: HEZEKIAH

Hezekiah became king of the southern kingdom of Judah at the same time a new king in Assyria (the kingdom that eventually conquered the northern kingdom, Israel) rose to power (727 BC). Hezekiah rebelled against him. He most likely stopped sending tribute and dignitaries to Nineveh, the capital, to demonstrate independence from Assyrian rule.[11] Nothing significant occurred as a result of his rebellion until several years after Samaria (the capital of Israel) was taken and the northern territory, Israel, dispersed.

Eventually, the Assyrian king attacked cities in the southern Judean territory and Hezekiah submitted to him, as Judah had done before. Hezekiah sent tribute, and vassals were taken to Nineveh. Shortly after Hezekiah humbled himself, the king of Assyria sent a message with three of his highest ranking commanders. Read 2 Kings 18:17–37 and describe the ominous situation below.

_____

_____

_____

_____

_____

Hezekiah was threatened, God was mocked, and the people were made very afraid. Now turn to Isaiah 37:14–20 and read Hezekiah's response. He did three things that we should do when we find ourselves in threatening situations and afraid. What was the first thing Hezekiah did after he read the letter (v. 14)?

_____

_____

The second thing Hezekiah did was pray. He acknowledged who God is and His sovereignty in supreme rule over all the earth. Then he asked the Lord to open His eyes and ears to hear the awful things the Assyrian king had said. "Did you hear what he said about you?" Hezekiah recounted.

Then Hezekiah told the Lord that the king of Assyria spoke the truth. The Assyrians _had_ destroyed every kingdom and trampled every other god. (Hezekiah recognized that those idols were not like his God.) In that moment of laying it all out before the Lord, exposing the bad guys, and asking for help, Hezekiah relinquished control of the situation and placed all his trust in his God.

What was God's response to this relinquishing and trusting (vv. 21, 33–35)?

_____

_____

_____

EXAMPLE #2: DANIEL

Daniel found himself in a similarly distressing predicament. The backstory can be read in Daniel 6:1–9. Basically, Daniel had lived a life above reproach in all areas. Some, out of jealousy and envy, found this despicable. They devised a plan to ensure Daniel's downfall, and all they could think of was catching him in prayer. They convinced the king to sign a law that prohibited prayer to any god besides the king or face the lions' den. Although you may be familiar with this narrative, please focus on how Daniel handled a situation completely out of his control.

Read Daniel 6:10–11. How was Daniel discovered?

_____

_____

In verses 12–16 we learn Daniel's horrifying reality. He had asked God to help him, and now he was headed for his death. Let that reality sink in. All Daniel could do was relinquish control and trust his God. This was _all_ he could do. No one could help him or reverse the situation. God took this opportunity to make himself known to a Persian government in a miraculous way (vv. 21–23). What reason was given for Daniel's condition (v. 23)?

_____

_____

Honestly, we are not promised a lion-taming miracle in the midst of our circumstances. Shadrach, Meshach, and Abednego understood this truth. These men refused to bow before an idol at the risk of death, just like Daniel. But when questioned by the king, they spoke of their theology, lived out in their reality:

> _If we are thrown into the blazing furnace, the God we serve_
> _is able to deliver us from it, and he will deliver us from Your_

> *Majesty's hand. But even if he does not, we want you to know,*
> *Your Majesty, that we will not serve your gods or worship the*
> *image of gold you have set up.*

Daniel 3:17–18

This is mental prowess—the kind of silent strength blazing forward in a victorious moment of **relinquishment**—with the only assurance being "I don't know what is going to happen, but I **trust** You with my very life."

EXAMPLE #3: JESUS

No other example can compare to that of Christ in the moments before His arrest:

> *Going a little farther, he fell to the ground and prayed that if*
> *possible the hour might pass from him. "Abba, Father," he said,*
> *"everything is possible for you. Take this cup from me. Yet not*
> *what I will, but what you will."*

Mark 14:35–36

Our Savior is crying out to His Father, pleading, "If there is any other way, Father, I want to take it! You can do ANYTHING! You can make another way! But if you don't . . . if this is the only option, I will crawl upon that wretched plank, endure the torture, the humiliation, and ultimate rejection by you, because I trust you. Thy will be done." This is the ultimate demonstration of *relinquishment* of self and the pinnacle of *trust*.

Jesus repeated this relinquishment of self and placement of trust at least three times (vv. 32, 39). How much more important for us to pray for the mental strength to fling ourselves upon that spiritual altar, not knowing how it's going to turn out—to say "I trust you" and to repeat this process as many times as it takes or until our dying breaths are silenced and He ushers us into His presence!

Let's start today. First, identify what is keeping you from flinging yourself upon the spiritual altar. Maybe you have practiced the fling many times before, but you keep pulling yourself off. What should you do to get back on?

_____

_____

_____

Maybe writing out your situation and physically spreading it out before the Lord would encourage you to leave it with Him. Or maybe you need to change your position, kneeling like Daniel. You might have situations in which a good exposé is in order. What do you need to do?

_____

_____

_____

_____

Today, begin to turn yourself and every situation over to Him. Determine to make *relinquishing* your habit until you no longer pick yourself back off that altar in complete *trust* of the God who loves you first.

Day 4

We Fix Our Gaze

Let your eyes look straight ahead; fix your gaze directly before
you. Give careful thought to the paths for your feet and be
steadfast in all your ways. Do not turn to the right or the left;
keep your foot from evil.

Proverbs 4:25–27

Yesterday we focused on the daily yielding of ourselves as living sacrifices. Relinquishing and trusting are the results of renewing our minds to reflect His desires for us and His ability to do what is best, and then walking in obedience. Today our focus turns to centering our minds on what is most important to us.

WORSHIP ALONE

Worship results when our thoughts focus on God and we demonstrate He *is* our favorite. We do this in a variety of ways and places. Some of us experience this focused communication in nature, alone. Others of us use music. We often live lives of service, giving ourselves to raising godly children and participating in various ministries. These too are worship.

Yet any time our attention is divided or we refuse to turn from our sin, relinquish control, or offer portions of our lives, God is aware. The Almighty suffers no fools. Just like He was on to the Israelites when they were stiff-necked (Deuteronomy 9:13), simply going through the motions (Isaiah 29:13–), and dividing their affections (1 Kings 18:21)—their worship was not only unacceptable, it was abhorrent to Him. Sadly, He knows when He *is not* our favorite.

David recognized the possible dangers of letting God fall from a place of supreme importance in his life. Write out Psalm 139:23.

_____

_____

_____

Now read Psalm 26:2–3:

Test me, Lord, and try me, examine my heart and my mind; for
I have always been mindful of your unfailing love and have
lived in reliance on your faithfulness.

Think about these verses and pen your own prayer below, giving God the freedom to penetrate into any secret place in your life and open those forbidden doors within your mind and heart.

_____

_____

_____

Right now, I'm asking the Holy Spirit to illuminate anything within us that is stealing our affections, making God less than our most treasured possession. It's possible you have become indifferent to the love of God. Maybe the affection and yearnings to serve Him that you once felt have cooled. Your worship has turned cold. List anything that comes to mind about your own mind and heart that could be affecting the acceptability of your worship. Remember, you are **His** treasure. He just wants to be **yours.**

_____

_____

_____

_____

WORSHIP TOGETHER

My new normal with eight kids ranging from kindergarten to high school age resembles the movie _Cheaper by the Dozen_ more often than I would like to admit. Every day is LOUD. At least four conversations are happening simultaneously at any given time. We no longer fit at one table. We consume Goldfish®, Chex Mix®, and animal crackers by the gallons. Most afternoons, the five elementary kids need constant help with homework, and everyone needs me to read with them and listen to them while I'm trying to prepare dinner for ten people before we move on to the next event. Someone invariably returns from school with ripped jeans, shoes that no longer fit, an animated tale of the latest girl drama, or a project requiring a minimum of two trips to Walmart that evening. Piles of unmatched dirty shoes lie by the door. Laundry spills out of the of laundry room at all times, and the garage currently houses only bikes, balls, cats, scooters, two freezers, and Green Machines—no cars. This is normal life at my house during the week. Imagine our house on a Sunday morning . . .

Sunday mornings, for many of us, can be more than frustrating. Often it's the day you are the most distracted and irritated and when the weirdest things go wrong, like the heel coming off a shoe, the dog having an accident, or the milk spilling across the entire kitchen floor. Sunday mornings seem to be the only time you are ever late. You discover problems with your clothes, the breakfast burns, and you suddenly realize nothing is left in the kitchen for lunch. Then, while driving to church, you discover you forgot to get gas! Now you are _really_ late. All hope of a worshipful spirit is gone.

Why does this happen? Because the enemy is jealous of our worship of God. He knows God wants to be our favorite. Satan understands that ultimately he loses the war, but he is not going to concede a single battle without a fight. Our enemy is smooth. He knows we are not going to choose the pitchfork-and-horns image of him, but also that we are so easily distracted, derailed, and unraveled within our own minds. Ours is a mental battle. We lose our focus. Our joy disappears from sight. If we are honest, we would admit that too often, by the time we arrive to corporate worship, we are completely distracted. So we carelessly sing words to familiar tunes, bow our heads emptily for prayer, and take mindless notes off the screen prompts while lost in our own concerns and frustrations. The time of worship passes, we gather our things, and we leave unchanged, empty, and utterly defeated.

Satan wants our worship. If we won't freely hand it over, he tries to steal it from the one it is due. Our enemy is so envious of the worship given to God that enticing Jesus to worship him was one of the three temptations he used against Him (Matthew 4:8–9).

What do Satan's attempts to steal your worship look like?

_____

_____

_____

Unfortunately, sin is sin. It doesn't matter how we arrive there, each of us is responsible before God for our sin. Anything less than centering on Him as our single focus in worship is sin.

FIXING OUR GAZE IN WORSHIP

What should worship look like?

> *"Worship in its truest sense takes place only when our full attention is on God—on His glory, power, majesty, love and compassion."*[12]

Read the following verses and note how Scripture describes what worship should look like:

Exodus 33:10

_____

_____

1 Kings 1:47–48

_____

_____

2 Chronicles 29:20–30

_____

_____

Psalm 95:6

_____

_____

Psalm 96:9

_____

_____

Psalm 100:1–5

_____

_____

Acts 13:1–2

_____

_____

Hebrews 12:28–29

> *Therefore, since we are receiving a kingdom that cannot be shaken, let us be thankful, and so worship God acceptably with reverence and awe, for our "God is a consuming fire."*

_____

_____

Revelation 4:10–11

> *The twenty-four elders fall down before him who sits on the throne and worship him who lives for ever and ever. They lay their crowns before the throne and say: "You are worthy, our Lord and God, to receive glory and honor and power, for you created all things, and by your will they were created and have their being."*

_____

_____

Think about these verses we have studied today. What should worship look like in your life when you fix your gaze on Him?

_____

_____

_____

_____

WHAT CAN WE DO TO MAKE OUR WORSHIP MORE WORSHIPFUL?

You and I can take an active role in transforming our worship. In fact, we must. The path of least resistance leads to heartless motions and bated distractions. May we no longer be willing participants in stealing worship from our King.

1. Prepare! Prepare! Prepare!

Centering begins the day *before* your worship service. Clean up the night before. Plan all three meals ahead of time and make them easy (be supermom or supergrandma another time). Eat on paper plates. Shower the night before. Lay out your clothes, and put gas in the car. List some preparations you can begin to make this week.

_____

_____

_____

2. Anticipate Recurrent Problems

One of my daughters often needs help with her hair at the very last minute. She has not mastered how long hair takes, and this causes the whole family to leave late. I have learned to avoid the problem by getting myself ready a few minutes earlier so I am available to help. What is something that invariably happens at your house? What can you do to combat this derailment?

_____

_____

_____

3. Position Yourself for Worship

Several years ago, I helped with a praise team during a contemporary service. Over time, changes occurred that left me perpetually irritated and disappointed. As I earnestly prayed about what to do, I heard that familiar voice in my head that I have come to recognize as the Holy Spirit, giving this pointed advice: "Cheri, My issue is not whether or not you have a microphone. Where are you going to worship me? Either stop it, and worship me up on the stage or stop it, and worship me from the pew. You decide." (Notice, my worship or lack thereof was my problem, not anyone else's). I got the point. It was time to step down to learn how to worship from the inside regardless of what was happening around me. I am accountable to God for my worship of Him. It's my responsibility to show Him that He *is* my favorite.

Is your worship position keeping you from focusing on Him? Remember, your lack of worship has nothing to do with music styles, song selection, volume, instruments, or the opinion you hold of those in your midst. You are accountable to God for your worship, just as I am accountable for mine. Where are you going to worship with a singleness of focus, pouring all your attention on Him?

_____

_____

_____

Position yourself there. Let Him know, unashamedly, that He *is* your favorite.

DAY 5

WE PERSEVERE IN ALL CIRCUMSTANCES

> *Therefore, my dear brothers and sisters, stand firm. Let nothing move you. Always give yourselves fully to the work of the Lord, because you know that your labor in the Lord is not in vain.*
>
> 1 Corinthians 15:58

If you are yearning to live out the Greatest Commandment, you are probably nearing exhaustion. Are you striving to love Him—really love Him? Are you battling to gain the victory within your mind? Are you patterning your life after those who have paved the way toward the kingdom, plowing full speed ahead rather than remaining satisfied with meandering in the general direction? God is showing you truth after revolutionary truth as you seek His face, so you keep after Him. But it's hard work, and sometimes you find yourself discouraged. Let's face it, living in wholehearted pursuit is *beyond* our maximum capacity.

DON'T QUIT

Today I invite you to step into the sandals of an Israelite taken to Babylon in captivity. You have lived as a captive for seventy years. It is the year 538 BC, and Cyrus the Great has come to power in Babylon. Believing God has given him the task of rebuilding the temple in Jerusalem (Ezra 1:1–4) Cyrus issues a proclamation that anyone desiring to leave Babylon and return to Jerusalem to help with the rebuilding of the temple may go. You and about four hundred thousand of your friends do!

> *Then the family heads of Judah and Benjamin, and the priests and Levites—everyone whose heart God had moved—prepared to go up and build the house of the LORD in Jerusalem.*
>
> Ezra 1:5

You and the other several hundred thousand Jews are so ecstatic that the journey, though long and arduous, is the most joyous trip imaginable. Many of you have never seen *home*. Everyone is talking about what it will be like. You can hardly believe it's actually happening! You are free! And all the promises of God (Jeremiah 29:10-14) are coming to fruition before your very eyes, just like He promised. Your God *IS* faithful. You cannot wait for the work to begin!

Two key leaders in the rebuilding and returning are Zerubbabel son of Shealtiel and Jeshua son of Jozadak. Zerubbabel is a descendent of the kings of Judah and serves as governor. Jeshua is the high priest. They work very well together, organizing the family records to determine what land belongs to whom, and in the restoration of worship (who is responsible for which task).

The records indicate where your family property lies. Along with your family and companions, you begin resettling what was once your family inheritance. It will be a lot of work, but you don't care. It's beautiful and it is yours.

Soon, Zerubbabel and Jeshua call everyone to assemble. The altar to the Lord is rebuilt, and the religious requirements are reinstated. It's incredible! Everything you've been told about Jehovah is true. The stories are true. The temple and worship are real. You bring your sacrifices and offerings. You give them gladly. Then Jeshua assigns you a specific job for beginning the work of rebuilding the actual temple. Within no time at all, the foundation is laid and there is a great celebration.

Pick up this narrative in Ezra 4:1–5. What happens next? And how long does this continue (v. 24)?

_____

_____

_____

It's hopeless. There is nothing you or any of your leadership can do. Each of you turn your energies to your own lives, and the temple foundation remains all that is completed on the temple for the next sixteen years. After a stalemate that long, all hope is gone of anything ever changing.

Now step out of your Jewish sandals and into your own. When was the last time you were discouraged from doing exactly what God had instructed you to do? When have you been made afraid to continue on?

_____

_____

_____

I know how you feel. These verses came directly off the pages of my journal. We call that recurrent crisis moment in my life Gazebo Time at my house. It's the day I just can't believe one more minute in what I cannot see. I toss my word from God into the imaginary trash can (because I probably just made it up). I am so stupid to think He could actually use me! And I head out to our gazebo in a distraught crying fit. Then, when my tears are dry and I reenter my life, all too often I have made a strategic error. I reenter *as if* I must not be able to hear God at all to have believed that absurd nonsense of impossibility. I leave my God-sized dreams outside and go about my regular, ordinary life.

That is exactly what the Jewish remnant did. They started living their regular lives and assumed they must have misunderstood the God-sized dreams of the past . . . until the second year of King Darius.

Read Haggai 1:1–4. Haggai had a word from the Lord for the governor, Zerubbabel, and the high priest, Jeshua. Basically, he asked them why they put their God-sized dream aside to pursue mediocrity. They were mistaken to have done so. Write out verse 5.

_____

_____

_____

Read verses 6–11. What was the problem?

_____

_____

I recorded these verses in my journal when I read them and related this situation to my own settling for mediocrity. I too was busy with my own house and had given up on the vision God had shown me for what He had planned for my life. This word from Haggai was a reprimand for Zerubbabel, Jeshua, and the people—and for me. Could it be one for you too? What is the state of your God-sized dream?

_____

_____

_____

_____

The people recognized the voice of the Lord through Haggai to get them back to the task of rebuilding the temple. They received the word and made the decision to be obedient. God uses this same word to get me back on track for believing Him. Read verses 13–15. What part of these verses is most precious to you?

_____

_____

_____

When the dream seemed too big and their abilities so limited, when the span of time with zero encouragement to complete the task seemed too great, the people became very discouraged.

They quit. They felt God had abandoned them with the unfulfilled promise.

Then just when they least expected it, Haggai, whose name appropriately means "the festive one"[13] showed up to encourage them with a word from Lord. God gave them exactly the assurances and encouragement they needed in His timing.

Read Haggai 2:1–19. Then write out the encouragement Haggai offered.

Verses 1–5

_____

_____

_____

Verses 6–9

_____

_____

_____

The people were poor and did not have the means to restore the temple to its previous glory. I love how God assures us we are not responsible to give what we do not have—only what He has entrusted to us.

Read Haggai 2:10–19 again. Complete verse 19:

"Is there any seed left in the barn? Until now, the vine and the fig tree, the pomegranate and the olive tree have not borne fruit.

'From _____.' "

Sweet friend, I do not know your situation. I cannot imagine what God has placed in your heart that has been left unfulfilled. I do, however, know how it hurts.

DON'T GIVE UP

Maybe you have walked away, like I have, out of discouragement. Let me remind you, He is with you and has come to bring you back. Your Gazebo Time is over. I don't know what the blessing will be, and I don't know when it will show up. What I do know is this: **the blessing is coming to you.**

Maybe there is no one in your life to encourage you. Be strong, sweet sister, and *do the work*, for He is with you. Trust His Word. He will do exactly what He promised.

The Holy Spirit is in you.

Do not be afraid.

Maybe you don't know what to do next . . .

Stand right there.

Let not your inconsistencies, inadequacies, or fatigue cause you to quit. Commit yourself to the God-sized task before you. He will see you through. I can imagine you might have some business with the Lord today, just the two of you.

_____

_____

_____

_____

_____

_____

_____

_____

_____

_____

ENDNOTES

1. Goodrick & Kohlenberger, *Zondervan NIV Exhaustive Concordance.*

2. Charles Spurgeon, *Sermons*, 9:322.

3. Ibid., 306.

4. John Piper, *Think!* (Wheaton: Crossway, 2010), 91.

5. W. E. Vine, *Vine's Expository Dictionary of Old and New Testament Words..* (Iowa: World Bible, 1981), 298.

6. Goodrick & Kohlenberger, *Zondervan NIV Exhaustive Concordance.*

7. A. T. Robertson, *Word Pictures*, 298.

8. Piper, *Think!*, 90.

9. Ibid.

10. Goodrick & Kohlenberger, *Zondervan NIV Exhaustive Concordance.*

11. G. Rawlinson, *The Pulpit Commentary*, H. D. M. Spence, Joseph S. Exell, eds. (Grand Rapids: Wm. B. Eerdmans, 1962), 5:359.

12. Franklin Graham, *Billy Graham in Quotes* (Nashville: Thomas Nelson, 2011), 381.'

13. W. J. Deane, *Pulpit Commentary*, 14:IV.

NOTES

LESSON 6

WHEN STRENGTH MOVES MOUNTAINS

Love the L<small>ORD</small> *your God with all your heart and with all
your soul and with all your strength.*

Deuteronomy 6:5

When I see the command to love the Lord with all my strength, the mental picture I hold is of a cartoon muscle-bound man, smiling under his four-thousand-pound barbells. As you can imagine, there is a disconnect understanding how I am supposed to love my God like this character. But when I learned the Hebrew word for strength, I began to connect the dots between the words on the page and what they should look like in my life.

The Hebrew word for strength is actually an adverb. It is "a marker of great degree or quantity used like the words: very, greatly, exceedingly, or much."[1] In other words, if all I can do, compared to my muscle-bound partner, is lift what would be as heavy as a couple of coconuts attached to a limbo stick, and I lift with absolute gusto, I am living out strength the way God intended. This is a clearer understanding of the true meaning of strength to me. Leave it to the Almighty to make this word about our own personal exertion, regardless of size and power, rather than paramount brute muscle.

God is looking for women to love Him with all their strength. He does not expect us to be bench-pressing babes any more than He desires us to be damsels in distress. He created women to be feminine but also to love Him with absolute gusto.

DAY 1

HE PROVIDES WHAT WE NEED

*She sets about her work vigorously;
her arms are strong for her tasks.*

Proverbs 31:17

Feminine strength differs from masculine strength. For example, a few weeks ago, my daughter threw up suddenly at a basketball game. Three women charged forward to help me. One, whom I hardly knew, was on her hands and knees cleaning up the vomit—which my husband later confided a man would scarcely do for anyone. Women, for the most part, don't even hesitate. We are not thinking about our outfits, the smell, or how gross the situation. Women stepped forward in an instant. **Strength** *in immediate and selfless aid.*

The ability to maneuver a stroller with a baby, a toddler, a shopping cart, and the remote to open the back hatch of your car is another classic. I watched a mom come out of the store like this and within minutes change the baby's diaper with one hand while getting what she needed out of her bags to wrap a present and then secure the toddler in the car seat and wrap the present in the back of her SUV, all the while keeping a hand on the baby. **Strength** *in dexterity and resourcefulness.*

My friend Lisa lives with a chronic, debilitating illness, but you would never know by observing her or talking with her. She exudes genuine joy. Refusing to let her health keep her from living, she pushes through immeasurable pain and internal suffering. **Strength** *in grit and tenacity.*

Female strength blazes through in other ways particular to our gender. I began my doctoral program eight months pregnant for fear that if I waited until our first baby arrived, I would never begin. Two years into my seven-year endeavor, another baby joined the Strange family. Teaching responsibilities at the university were combined with scheduling classes around Mother's Day Out and a sweet teen babysitter. Sleep, quality meals, and clean floors were not top priorities during this season. I was pulled in too many directions. Never did I feel I did anything well. Although I knew this combination of tasks was exactly what God called me to do and when, it was extremely difficult to do everything at once.

The details will be different, but you and I likely find common ground in this area. Most women I know (married, single, young, and older) do five things simultaneously while we are thinking about another—thus the invention of the minivan. (Glory to God!)

God designed women to approach life with all the file drawers open and to engage holistically. Studies show we do multiple tasks simultaneously 70 percent more effectively than the other gender.[2] We are to do what God's called us to do in the midst of doing the other three things He's called us to do. This requires strength *beyond* what you and I possess. If God's desire is for us to love Him with every ounce of our strength—*absolute gusto*—then how do we keep all of the God-ordained penguins on the iceberg? What does it look like to love God with everything we are to such a degree that there is nothing left to give without life completely falling to pieces around us in the process?

TAKE AN ENERGY ASSESSMENT

Sometime we find ourselves completely spent because we are too heavily involved in things that we never really asked the Lord if we should pursue. Good opportunities? Yes. Exactly what God has called us to do right now? *Not necessarily.* Giving our pursuits a thorough assessment is essential. These are tough questions to ponder, but ponder we must. Is that hobby worth the time and money right now? Has He instructed you to work full-time for this season of life, or was that *your* idea? Are we using the need for me-time as a justification for countless hours of temporary enjoyment? Are these the ministry areas He wants us to do right now? Could it be time to relinquish some responsibilities to expend our energies on God's dreams for us instead of our own?

Is there anything the Holy Spirit brings to mind that you should reassess about where you expend your energy?

_____

_____

Other times we're too busy because God has issued an unreasonable amount of responsibility. We know what we are to do. It's simply too much for one person to accomplish. But sometimes, this is His way. Notice the load of responsibility given to Eleazar as well as the burden Moses carried:

> *Eleazar son of Aaron, the priest, is to have charge of the oil for the light, the fragrant incense, the regular grain offering and the anointing oil. He is to be in charge of the entire tabernacle and everything in it, including its holy furnishings and articles.*
>
> Numbers 4:16

> *I cannot carry all these people by myself; the burden is too heavy for me.*
>
> Numbers 11:14

I can relate to Moses. I have prayed these words more than once. List all the things you believe God has ordained for your life in this season. Be as detailed as you like. (I realize some of you will need the rest of the entire page. Write small!)

_____

_____

_____

_____

Think about those pillars in Scripture who were given monumental responsibilities: Moses, bringing the people of God out of Egypt and leading them to the Promised Land; David, conquering nations, establishing a kingdom, and planning the temple; Esther, saving the Jewish people; Nehemiah, a cupbearer turned ruins-restorer and governor; and Paul, missionary to the entire known world. How did they succeed? How were they able to expend every ounce of energy managing the responsibilities God placed upon their lives without trying to do it all themselves? How did they distinguish what was significant from what was not? Why were they able to live in faith rather than disbelief and allow God the freedom to do marvelous wonders before their very eyes? They had a balance for which we strive.

Honestly, if I could discover that balance, infusing it into daily living, I would achieve my calling. Everything God wants me to accomplish would get done. No matter when the day came, my body would wear out at the perfect time. My life would have been spent on the one who loves me more than I can possibly fathom, fulfilling His purposes, His way, in His time. Where does the strength to love God with everything we are, while bringing out captives, conquering foes, rebuilding ruins, and tirelessly spreading the good news, begin?

STRENGTH BEGINS WITH STRENGTH

What is unique about the following verses?

> *But You, O Lord, be not far off; O my Strength, come quickly to help me.*
>
> Psalm 22:19, NIV 1984

O my Strength, I sing praise to you; you, O God,
are my fortress, my loving God.

Psalm 59:17, NIV 1984

_____

_____

_____

Strength is part of God's character. Like love (1 John 4:16), Jealous (Exodus 34:14), or Redeemer (Isaiah 60:16), the name Strength defines who He is. Could it be that God asks us to love Him with all *our* strength because it's one more facet for understanding Him who loves us? Remember, we serve a relational God who greatly desires us to know Him (Jeremiah 9:23–24). What does it mean to you that God himself is the **person of Strength** as well as the **source of strength** for your life?

_____

_____

_____

Read 1 Chronicles 16:11 in your Bible and then Isaiah 33:2. When is this power available to us?

O Lord, be gracious to us; we have waited [expectantly] for You.
Be the arm [of Your servants—their strength and defense] every
morning, our salvation in the time of trouble.

Isaiah 33:2, AMP

_____

_____

Read 2 Chronicles 16:9 and Isaiah 40:10. To what degree is God interested in giving us His strength?

_____

_____

The lifelong lesson for us is to rely on God for strength at all times. We need His strength for our everyday chaos as well as the cataclysmic moments of crisis.

WE NEED STRENGTH FOR EVERY DAY

David is a perfect example for daily life. What can we learn from the following psalms?

Psalm 18:32

_____

_____

Psalm 29:11

The LORD gives strength to his people;
the LORD blesses his people with peace.

_____

_____

Isaiah 58:11

> The LORD *will guide you always; he will satisfy your needs in a*
> *sun-scorched land and will strengthen your frame.*

_____

_____

1 Peter 4:11

_____

_____

WE NEED STRENGTH IN EVERY CRISIS

King Jehoshaphat, son of Asa (and one of the better kings of Judah), met with a crisis. A vast army was coming against him. Read in 2 Chronicles 20:2–12 how Jehoshaphat handled the situation. If you were to do something like Jehoshaphat did (similar to verse 12), what would you say to God?

_____

_____

_____

Years later, Nehemiah faced strong and constant opposition to rebuilding the wall around Jerusalem. Read in Nehemiah 6:8–9 how he handled the crisis. What was his solution?

_____

_____

_____

WE RECEIVE STRENGTH IN DIFFERENT WAYS

God uses different means to strengthen His people. According to the following verses, in what ways can we receive His strength?

1 Samuel 23:14–18

_____

_____

Luke 22:43

_____

_____

Romans 4:20–21

> *Yet he did not waver through unbelief regarding the promise of God, but was strengthened in his faith and gave glory to God, being fully persuaded that God had power to do what he had promised.*

_____

_____

Ephesians 3:14–16

_____

_____

Colossians 2:7

_____

_____

2 Thessalonians 2:16–17

> *May our Lord Jesus Christ himself and God our Father, who loved us and by his grace gave us eternal encouragement and good hope, encourage your hearts and strengthen you in every good deed and word.*

_____

_____

Hebrews 13:9

_____

_____

WHAT CAN WE DO TO INCREASE OUR RECEPTION OF GOD'S STRENGTH?

Our God designed us to grow in His strength. You and I can follow the lead of those who understood more, achieved more, endured more, and suffered more than any amount of human fortitude could explain. He is ready to impart. We simply need to prepare to receive.

1. Bend the Knee

This has been the practice of those who loved God completely. Their lives demonstrated their affections by their posture. I know of no better way to receive the strength we desperately need today and during times of crisis than to follow this example. There is something about bending our knee before the God of the universe that cannot be accomplished any other way. I chose to write this chapter with my computer on the couch and my knees to the ground, because this task is beyond my abilities. If there was power to be accessed from the God who is Strength that could be fitted onto a laptop while an unqualified nobody typed her heart away, I did not want to miss it.

2. Ask for It

We have numerous examples of those who asked and received. This one epitomizes our lesson today. Hear the emotion. Sense the urgency and desperate cry for a constant supply of more strength to love God with every ounce of our being while doing exactly what He has called us to do.

> At once the father of the boy gave [an eager, piercing, inarticulate] cry with tears, and he said, LORD, I believe! [Constantly] help my weakness of faith.
>
> Mark 9:24, AMP

In light of what the Holy Spirit has spoken to you through God's Word, what would you pray today?

_____

_____

_____

_____

_____

_____

_____

_____

_____

DAY 2

HE EXPECTS COOPERATION

Yesterday we focused on God as our Strength. We can take His strength upon ourselves in daily living as well as for any and every critical moment we encounter. Today and tomorrow we turn toward our personal responsibilities in loving God with every ounce of power we can muster. The Proverbs 31 woman is a perfect example. She is praised for her strength as well as her efforts to cultivate _more_ spiritual, mental, and physical strength. Each of us, regardless of health, size, or weight, can increase our personal strength to love God with our full potential.

> She girds herself with strength [spiritual, mental, and physical fitness for her God-given task] and makes her arms strong and firm.
>
> Proverbs 31:17, AMP

Each of us has God-given tasks that require more of us physically, mentally, and spiritually than we possess. Yes, we look to Him to do what only He can do, but the Bible is clear that we have a responsibility to cooperate. We are to get ourselves ready to meet the challenges God has designed in advance for us and to build up our bodies to stand against anything the enemy throws our way.

Read Psalm 119:28 and finish this sentence:

Strengthen me according _____

_____

_____ .

The Hebrew word for *strength* in Psalm 119:28 means "to get up, arise, stand, establish; confirm, and restore."[3] How do you think the psalmist expects the Word of God to strengthen him?

_____

_____

_____

Read Ephesians 6:10–17. This passage calls us to two actions. What are they (vv. 10–11)?

_____

_____

Scholars believe Paul's ordering of these actions is intentional. We must first be strong in the Lord and in His mighty power *before* we can put on the full armor of God. What does it mean to be strong in the Lord? It means to meditate on Him and His strength.[4] It means we are to allow God's Word to permeate our minds as we read it. It means we cannot squeeze it in with one hand on our phone and the other jotting things down on our to-do lists as they pop into our minds while we do our due diligence. Thinking about His greatness and what He is saying through the Word enables us to become strong.

Complete the diagram on the following page using Ephesians 6:14–17 to illustrate how Paul encourages us to be strong by putting on the full armor of God. Be sure to identify six essential components Paul identifies. Star the areas that you believe most need strengthening in your life today.

The armor works together to protect us and help us be victorious against what we cannot see. Notice we are given *one* offensive weapon against the enemy: God's Word. We can't stop the flaming arrows from coming at us, but we can strengthen our position against the enemy. When we infuse the Word into our minds and hearts, it becomes part of our fiber. It begins to slip off our tongues when we pray. Eventually the Word takes up residence and become who we are. The Word of God literally makes us stronger and more difficult to tangle with, but not if it remains unencountered in the pages of our Bibles.

GO ON OFFENSE WITH THE WORD

Women tell me how they just cannot memorize Scripture. They have tried, but it doesn't stick. Based upon a parable Jesus told about the enemy snatching the Word from hearers (Matthew 13:19), there may some legitimacy to this feeling of doom. The enemy also understands how we grow in strength, and he does not want us becoming stronger opponents. If you feel like your efforts to memorize the Word are fruitless, be encouraged. Satan knows that if he allows you to get God's Word in your head, you just might beat the sinister pants off him.

It's time to get to work. You don't need to go looking for some kind of system that teaches you how to memorize. Your brain works fine. Get a note card. Write the verse. Or grab your phone and download an app. (My friends like Fighter Verses.) Say your verse over and over and over. If that does not work, do it again. Like throwing mud on a chain-link fence, eventually, as a little bit dries, more and more of the mud will begin to stick. Find yourself someone to whom you can be accountable. If we are going to become stronger, we must know the Word of God.

Read Deuteronomy 11:8. In addition to getting the Word inside us, what does this verse suggest makes us stronger?

_____

_____

The Hebrew word for *strength* in Deuteronomy 11:8 means "to establish oneself firmly; to encourage, to rally strength; from the base meaning of physical hardness come by extension; physical and internal strength of character."[5] There remains a seamless connection between knowing God's Word and obeying Him in every element of life, including the strength we possess. God has much for us to do for His name and His glory. Our first training ground for increasing our personal strength lies not at the gym but in our diligence to know His Word and follow it.

GET YOURSELF READY

The second priority is to get ourselves ready to do whatever He calls us to do. This can take on myriad options and appearances. Let's look at a few examples in Scripture.

Read 2 Samuel 22:30–37. These verses form part of the song David composed after God delivered him from Saul. David acknowledges who is ultimately responsible for any victory he experiences, yet he also understands his personal responsibility. List what David attributes to God for his successes and what David's responsibilities were in order to be prepared to do everything God planned for him.

What God Helped David Accomplish	David's Responsibilities for Success

_____

_____

_____

_____

_____

> *He trains my hands for battle; my arms can bend a*
> *bow of bronze.*
>
> 2 Samuel 22:35

The Hebrew word for *trains* is a verb that means "to teach, instruct, and to cause to learn with the implication that the learning will be put to use."[6]

David didn't wait idly by for God to do what He promised. Before God brought David's call to fruition, David worked at becoming everything God dreamed him to become. Time after time, the challenge was beyond his ability (Psalm 18). He was faced with insurmountable odds, but David did not sit in a corner and bawl because God had yet to show His faithfulness. He took his sword and his muscle-bound body and pushed back his enemies with the supernatural aid of his God, until God's promises became his reality.

Is there anything you could be doing to prepare for whatever God has called you to do?

_____

_____

_____

Read Joshua 1:1–2 and circle what God tells Joshua to do:

> *After the death of Moses the servant of the LORD, the LORD said*
> *to Joshua son of Nun, Moses' aide:*
> *"Moses my servant is dead. Now then, you and all these people,*
> *get ready to cross the Jordan River into the land I am about to*
> *give to them—to the Israelites."*

Sometimes God tells us to get ready but leaves out the specifics of exactly *what* we are supposed to do AND *how* we are going to get across our Jordan River. Read Jeremiah 1:4–19. In verse 17, what does God tell Jeremiah to do?

_____

_____

What do you think God intended Jeremiah to do, in order to be ready?

_____

_____

The Hebrew word for _ready_ means "to gird up," "to take action" of various kinds, or the action of wrapping a belt around the waist.[7]

Is it is time for you to get ready? Do you know what to do? If you are not sure, stick with the last instructions He gave. We have a Straight and Narrow Policy at our house: stick to the last thing God told you until He tells you something new. What happens to me is that I get confused, and that familiar hindrance of fear returns. I simply want to quit. I set God's agenda aside to pursue my own.

Luke 12:35–48 is instructive in my case. What does this parable communicate about the importance of getting ready?

_____

_____

_____

What are the consequences if you and I choose *not* to get ready (v. 47)?

_____

_____

_____

Lord, let us not set your desires for our lives aside, but help us see clearly what you want us to do to get ready for whatever you have planned since the beginning of time. Show us how to grow stronger in your Word and in our obedience to you. Strengthen us to love you more.

DAY 3

WE TAKE ONE MORE STEP

> *Even youths shall faint and be weary, and . . . young men shall feebly stumble and fall exhausted.*
>
> Isaiah 40:30, AMP

Sometimes loving God with all our strength simply means that we **take one more step**. When our strength is gone and we have spent our time on our knees, one more step can seem insurmountable. When we have prepared well and have walked as far as we can, one more step is not as easy as it sounds. I'm thankful there are examples in Scripture that capture our human condition.

Please read all of 1 Kings 18. Meet Elijah, whose name means "The Lord is my God."[8] What a fitting testimony to bear during the time in which he ministered! Although little is known about his background, we learn from 2 Kings 1:8 that Elijah generally wore a garment of haircloth and a belt around his waist. He was known to appear and disappear suddenly (1 Kings 18:12), and he's believed to have been the head teacher for the other prophets during this time (2 Kings 2:7, 16–18). King Ahab and his wife, Jezebel (Elijah's contemporaries), hated him because of her affections for Baal worship. During Ahab's reign, Elijah was used by God to orchestrate a great display of His power against Baal and the killing of 450 priests of Baal (1 Kings 18:19–40). He was God's mouthpiece for announcing droughts (1 Kings 17:1) as well as calling them to a close (1 Kings 18:1). He served God with vigor and courage regardless of the circumstances or obvious risk. With the hand of the Lord upon him, Elijah was able to outrun a chariot in a fifteen-mile journey (1 Kings 18:46). Clearly, he was a disciplined man of strength, physically and spiritually.

First Kings 19 presents a different view of Elijah. Read 1 Kings 19:1–3. What is the cause of his flight?

_____

_____

What? The great Elijah, who under God's direction just orchestrated the most awesome God-contest of all time? The prophet who single-handedly eliminated the priests and prophets of Baal and distinguished the true God from an imitation? And then gave word of long-awaited rainfall and just outran a chariot?

We find Elijah in chapter 19 running from a woman. Fear motivated his flight, but there is more to Elijah's fleeing. In verses 4–5, what else do we learn?

_____

_____

Have you ever found yourself in a similar predicament? If so, describe the circumstances.

_____

_____

_____

There are times in the course of living that we come to a state of exhaustion. Elijah was _more_ than exhausted; he was despondent. He had had all he could take. The actual Hebrew rendering of "_I have had enough_" (NIV) is "Let it be enough."[9] All the mighty works and superhuman feats performed by the Lord through Elijah had been to no avail. The people were unchanged; the diabolical queen, undaunted.

Like Elijah, there are moments when _we_ have had it. We cannot take another step or serve another person. We have no more offers of godly advice to render. Our spirits are spent; our bodies, wearied. We need to sleep about six months.

Read verses 6–8. What do God's treatment of Elijah and the provision given to him suggest about God's opinion of Elijah's flight?

_____

_____

At this point, Elijah has fled to safety in Beersheba, the home of the true priests and prophets, under the protection of Jehoshaphat, king of Judah. Yet the angel tells him (v. 7) that the journey is too great and he needs more nourishment to endure. It is after this second encounter Elijah begins his forty-day journey.

Now read verses 8–18 and Exodus 33:21–22. What is significant about the location to which Elijah fled?

_____

_____

Elijah did not stay in just any cave on the mountain; he was in the cave thought to be the cleft in the rock where Moses stood while the glory of the Lord passed by.[10] God didn't tell Elijah where to go, nor did He chastise him for running. What if God's supernatural provision of nourishment, sleep, and a long journey away from danger was **THE PLAN** for Elijah's preservation and continued ministry?

Compare Elijah's escape from sure death to Saul's predicament in Acts 9:19–25. What commonalities do you find?

_____

_____

_____

Focus for a moment on the exchange between Elijah and God in 1 Kings 19:13–18. Why do you think God asked him the same question again?

_____

_____

_____

If we were to reword Elijah's lament to God, it might sound like this:

> *"Lord, I've been faithful to do everything you have asked of me. I've done it to the best of my abilities and beyond. My life has been lived for you in wholehearted devotion, regardless of the cost, as best I know how. However, NO ONE has listened or paid any attention. To no avail have I labored for you! I have seen no fruit, and I am so alone. To you is the only place I know to run. That's why I'm here."*

Can you relate to Elijah? When was the last time at least some of these could have been your words? Have you ever been so desperate for a glimpse of God's hand in your life that you were willing to do whatever you needed to do (even go without food) and go wherever you needed to go? Is this where you are today?

_____

_____

_____

Again, did God chastise Elijah? No. He came down from heaven to meet this man in his darkest hour of need, like He did with Moses, who also needed Him on that mountain (Exodus 33; 34:1–9).

God knew Elijah needed Him. We see God move heaven and earth for this man to be encouraged. He is **not** forgotten. He is **not** alone. God met him with the perfect balance of mercy, purpose, and sovereignty. Elijah was instructed to go back. "Get back in there, Elijah." God also gave him the task of anointing kings, which communicated that the troubles Elijah saw that day in Israel would soon come to an end. God would prevail over wickedness. He then acknowledged Elijah's loneliness by instructing him to anoint Elisha as his replacement.

Finally, he set the record straight with some statistics of His own: not *one* lonely prophet named Elijah but *seven thousand* people in Israel had not bowed to Baal. In other words, God was watching out for His own glory. We simply are not always privileged to see the big picture.

God knows you and I need Him too. At times when we are absolutely exhausted and despondent, He is our refuge.

> *But those who wait for the Lord [who expect, look for, and hope in Him] shall change and renew their strength and power; they shall lift up their wings and mount up [close to God] as eagles [mount up to the sun]; they shall run and not be weary, they shall walk and not faint or become tired.*
>
> Isaiah 40:31, AMP

Listen for His voice. Take one more step, straight into His arms.

DAY 4

WE BUILD UP THE BODY

I am not an athlete. You would recognize me as a child: always the girl sitting on the bench of the B team. Never was I out front, pushing my limits or winning any ribbons. But sometime between my teen years and adulthood, I discovered the psychological and calorie-burning benefits of jogging. Running allows me to release the stress of my day and keeps me relatively fit. The more stress-filled my life becomes, the greater my need to make time for this activity. In fact, a few years ago I faced an emotional crisis that a routine jog couldn't remedy, so I trained for and completed a marathon. Me, the bench sitter with no physical drive! Before you become too impressed, please note: I was passed by thousands of people, including two power-walking women (at least fifteen years my senior) having the best conversation about mile twenty-two, while I panted for my very life!

Of the many lessons that particular experience taught, I learned I could do more with my body than I ever dreamed possible. To my surprise, greater strength was available to *me*—the squatty-body nonathlete—when I simply disciplined myself toward the goal. For the first time, I had to give everything I could muster. The final three or four miles were so trying, I could not decide what my body needed to do: walk, fall to the ground, go to the bathroom, or just cry. I had spent all I had. Tears burned my eyes as I crossed that finish line because there was nothing left, and I caught a glimpse of what it looks like to love God with *all* my strength.

Paul draws a striking picture using a similar analogy in 1 Corinthians 9:24–27. Read these verses. In the passage, Paul makes a comparison between training for a physical race and the Christian's pursuit of Christ. What do you suppose Paul is suggesting? What might it look like for a Christian to *"run in such a way as to get the prize"* (NIV)?

_____

_____

_____

> *Everyone who competes in the games goes into strict training. They do it to get a crown that will not last; but we do it to get a crown that will last forever.*
>
> 1 Corinthians 9:25

According to Paul, both pursuits require strict training. What does strict training for pursuing Christ look like?

_____

_____

I tend to assume an exclusive spiritual training, yet Paul testifies to striking his body to make it his slave (v. 27), which communicates a physical-training element in complete devotion to Christ.

Look at the following verses. What is the key instruction given in each one?

Deuteronomy 31:6

_____

_____

1 Chronicles 28:10

_____

_____

2 Chronicles 15:7

_____

_____

Psalm 27:14

_____

_____

Haggai 2:4

_____

_____

We can find the command to be strong across the entire writ of Scripture. The problem is that each year you and I grow weaker unless we work at growing stronger. The physical properties at work in the universe and our bodies are in a constant state of running down. If we have any hope of being strong when strength is needed, and if we have any inclination to run to win, we need to build up our physical bodies.

WHAT IS THE STATE OF OUR STRENGTH?

> *She sets about her work vigorously;*
> *her arms are strong for her tasks.*
>
> Proverbs 31:17

Ask yourself, "Are my arms strong enough for my tasks?"

_____

Let's see, I have eight kids, including twin boys; the call of ministry on my life; and a husband who deserves more of me than whatever is left at the end of the day. I definitely need a stronger body just to keep pace with the parameters God has set for my life. Sometimes I feel like the writer of Psalm 22:15:

My strength is dried up like a potsherd. . . .

NIV, 1984

The Hebrew word for *strength* in this verse refers to power, might, ability, and often physical strength and the vigor of good health. It sometimes simply refers to the ability to accomplish an action.[11] How would you rate your strength today? Mark your present condition on this continuum:

Strong as an ox   *Weak as dried-up pottery*

I am in a season when I need to increase my discipline to eat more healthfully, drink more water, run faster and more often, and sleep more. I have been busy, and life has been a little more stressful. We have celebrated some holiday or someone's birthday almost every week for three months. That is a lot of cake and meals out. Snacking while I write is another habit I enjoy. After sitting at the desk writing for months at a time, my jeans begin to fit more snugly.

When my discipline in these areas deteriorates, I notice other areas in my life also relax. My house is messier. The clean laundry never quite makes it to the closet. I stop minding that my bed is left unmade. Our home office acquires piles and piles of paperwork I never seem to go through. If I stop to look around, I feel a little discouraged with how far I have allowed my disciplined life to stray, and it shows in my short-tempered attitude. Then I remind myself that life didn't succumb to this condition in a day, and one power hour will not undo it.

Maybe you have acquiesced to a similar predicament. Where should we begin? What does the writer of Hebrews suggest?

Hebrews 12:12

_____

_____

The Greek word for *strengthen* calls us to restore and to rebuild.[12]

WE RESTORE ORDER AND REBUILD

The following are suggestions for restoring order to our lives:

- Time with the Lord is a nonnegotiable. This is our first line of strength to restore.
- Focus on sleep and water intake.
- Select the main room in which you and your family gather and determine to keep it uncluttered.
- Drop one indulgence contributing to the snug jeans.
- Exercise one extra time this week (whether that means moving from zero sessions to one or from three days to four, etc.).
- Memorize a verse (pick an easy one).
- Let everything else remain disorderly.

In a couple of weeks, we can strive to take control of another room. I will work toward slimming down on the snacking and keeping the indulgences away. I will memorize another verse and finish the laundry. You and I need to work to take back our surroundings, our bodies, and our emotional stamina—step by intentional step.

What will your intentional steps look like this week? Take a minute to make a plan of restoration before you move on.

-
-
-
-
-
-
-
-

I have a dear friend who needs more physical strength today. Her needs are more intense than the average person's. She is a strong woman—a shining example of a steel magnolia. This is an accomplished professional who has beat back cancer and anything else standing in the way of living a full life. She recently retired from her career to move closer to the hospital. Doctors are treating her most recent bout with cancer by prescribing a chemotherapy pill for the next five years. This treatment with its side effects brings the possibility of taking a toll on my strong friend. Changing a few habits and curbing a sweet tooth are not going to touch her needs for greater strength.

According to Ezekiel 34:16, what does the Word promise my friend and anyone else in dire need of a stronger body?

_____

_____

The Hebrew word for *strengthen* in this verse means "to grasp, seize, hold; to make repairs; to give strength, repair, and encourage."[13]

WE HELP OTHERS FIND STRENGTH

You and I have a responsibility to come alongside people in our lives needing more strength. What can we learn from the following verses?

Deuteronomy 3:28

_____

_____

1 Samuel 23:14–18

_____

_____

Romans 15:1

_____

_____

2 Timothy 4:16–17

_____

_____

If there is someone in your life who needs to find strength in the Lord through you, what is the Holy Spirit nudging you to do? What would be an encouragement to your strong friend who desperately needs it?

_____

_____

_____

You and I need more physical strength. Statistically, our culture (within and outside the church) is filled with weak-bodied individuals consuming large portions of fat-saturated foods coupled with sedentary entertainment and spectator sports. But we are to be different. The kingdom needs stronger women. You and I must work at increasing our strength (Isaiah 35:3), stretch as far as we can go (1 Corinthians 9:27), trust Him to meet us in that place that leaves us completely spent, and fulfill His purposes for us (Psalm 57:2).

> He will keep you strong to the end, so that you will be blameless
> on the day of our Lord Jesus Christ. God, who has called you
> into fellowship with his Son Jesus Christ our Lord,
> is faithful.

1 Corinthians 1:8–9, NIV 1984

> Let the weakling say, "I am strong!".

Joel 3:10

> I can do all things through Christ who gives me strength.

Philippians 4:13, NIV 1984

DAY 5

WE TAKE OUR INHERITANCE

> Abram believed the Lord,
> and he credited it to him as righteousness.

> He also said to him, "I am the LORD, who brought you out of Ur
> of the Chaldeans to give you this land to take possession of it"

Genesis 15:6–7

Notice the two prepositional phrases in the last line of these verses.

Who is giving the land? _____

Who is taking possession? _____

God still desires our cooperation in becoming all He dreams us to become. Believing God will do what only He can do is paramount (v. 6). But then God keeps talking: *"He also said to him . . ."* (v. 7). God requires participation to fully possess that which is a gift. Abram could believe God about giving him an heir from his own body because he chose to trust in His strength to do the impossible. Abram could do nothing to make it happen but had to leave it in God's strong hands. However, Abram and his descendants would not be able to sit back and watch God be awesome when it came to taking possession of the Promised Land. God said to the Israelites through Moses:

> *"Take possession of the land and settle in it, for I have given you the land to possess."*
>
> Numbers 33:53

By God's design, taking possession of the gift would require old-fashioned belief in action through blood, sweat, and tears. Like the Israelites in the desert, we will not meander effortlessly into our inheritance. God expects our cooperation to possess all He has lovingly given us. Once again, possession is going to require every ounce of strength we can muster—and more. But oh, how it will be worth it!

> *"What no eye has seen, what no ear has heard, and what no human mind has conceived"—the things God has prepared for those who love him."*
>
> 1 Corinthians 2:9

WHAT EXACTLY ARE WE TO POSSESS?

The patriarchs, all the way down to the stiff-necked complainers Moses led, were looking toward entering and possessing a land flowing with milk and honey. It was to be a land with wheat and barley, vines and fig trees, pomegranates, olive oil, and honey, a land where bread would not be scarce and where the Israelites would lack nothing (Deuteronomy 8:8–9). They were to displace ten nations (greater and stronger than they): the lands of the Kenites, Kenizzites, Kadmonites, Hittites, Perizzites, Rephaites, Amorites, Canaanites, Girgashites, and Jebusites—and take their cities and their houses (Genesis 15:19–21).

Maybe you have physical land to fight for and possess by God's design. The Middle East remains a hot spot for claiming boundaries and displacing people. Most of us in Western civilization have difficulty relating to this kind of physical overthrow of nations. We have no enemies lurking behind walled cities to conquer or houses to occupy. However, we can relate to the promise of a good land in which we will lack nothing. We can understand facing insurmountable obstacles standing between us and what we believe the Word to speak over our lives. With these thoughts in place, let us turn to the New Testament. As believers in Christ Jesus, what is it you and I are to possess? What does the Promised Land look like this side of the New Testament?

Read 1 Corinthians 1:1–9. Who Paul is addressing this letter?

Now note every gift God has given to Paul's audience and list these below. (Hint: there are at least four.)

_____

_____

_____

Now read Ephesians 1:1–12. List any additional blessings given to those in Christ Jesus. Can you find at least six?

_____

_____

_____

_____

_____

According to John 15:8, what kind of life will bring glory to the Father?

_____

_____

Now imagine what your life would look like if you took possession of these gifts and responsibilities today. Write a description of you possessing your inheritance.

_____

_____

_____

_____

The reality is many of us do not live in our spiritual promised lands. We do not possess the gifts lavishly given to us; therefore, we do not stick our necks out to do what God has called us to do. The average Christian is not presently living a profoundly effective life for the kingdom.

It's time to start taking that which we have been given.

HOW DO WE TAKE POSSESSION OF OUR INHERITANCE?

Today we can decide to live differently. We can abandon our own safe havens of ineffectiveness to embrace the better legacy of kingdom building. Let's examine steps we can take to begin possessing that which we've already been given.

1. Accept the Gifts

The first step in taking our spiritual inheritance is to accept the gifts outlined in the verses we just read in Ephesians and First Corinthians. Think about your own life. Which of the gifts articulated in these verses would help you believe God loves you specifically?

_____

_____

Which of the gifts, if you really believed you could possess them, would make you stronger?

_____

Which of the gifts, if you really believed you could possess them, could give you the courage to step out to believe God would call you to do what you think He is calling you to do?

_____

Which of the gifts, if you really believed you could possess them, would be the exact equipping needed to do what God is calling you to do?

_____

Which of the gifts, if you really believed you could possess them, could enable you to be exceedingly effective in the life God has designed just for you?

_____

The woman described above is beginning to live out the full and fruit-filled life God dreams for her—*and she's soon to be you.*

2. Step Out into the Water

Read Joshua 3:7–13. Joshua was about to lead all Israel over the Jordan to take Jericho. The priests were to step into the water before anything miraculous occurred. Sometimes taking possession of our spiritual inheritances requires the same courage. It may be a phone call you are afraid to make. Maybe it is an interest meeting for fostering children. Or maybe there is a continuous nudging in your heart about something that requires you to go stand in the middle of a spiritual river at flood stage before anyone else follows.

Is the Holy Spirit at work in you, drawing you to step out into the water, so to speak, as a means for taking your God-given spiritual inheritance? What do you think He is leading toward today?

_____

_____

_____

_____

3. Clear the Trees

Read Joshua 17:14–18. Have you ever found yourself whining and wishing you had more spiritual responsibility but chickening out of taking that next step of faith? Maybe the obstacles looked too impossible to surmount? Maybe you could not see yourself fulfilling that role successfully? Maybe you simply didn't want to do the hard work required to operate within the expanded boundaries God wanted to give you?

What if you began today to take possession of everything God has given you? If this is where you find yourself on your journey toward taking possession of your spiritual inheritance, what might you need to do next?

_____

_____

_____

_____

The sad reality for the generation of Israelites charged with taking their physical inheritances was that they didn't succeed (Joshua 18:1–3). The country was brought under their control, but there were still tribes who had not yet received their inheritance. So Joshua said:

> *How long will you wait before you begin to take possession*
> *of the land that the LORD, the God of your ancestors,*
> *has given you?*

> Joshua 18:3

Just in case you struggle with the math, only five had taken possession, including the ones who had settled for the east side of the Jordan. And these tribes had not been completely successful:

> *Yet the Manassites were not able to occupy these towns, for the*
> *Canaanites were determined to live in that region.*

> Joshua 17:12

Excuse me? This was not God's plan. God gave the Israelites the land **to take possession of it** (Genesis 15:7; Numbers 33:53). Each tribe was allotted its own inheritance. But they never took possession of what they had been given, just like we often do not. Joshua encouraged the people just before he died:

> *The LORD your God himself will push them out for your sake.*
> *He will drive them out before you, and you will take possession*
> *of their land, as the LORD your God promised you.*

> Joshua 23:5

How does this verse encourage you toward taking your spiritual inheritance?

_____

_____

_____

4. Conquer That Which Could Not Be Conquered

The Promised Land remained fractured and not fully possessed until David came on the scene. God systematically redeemed the land through this man who loved Him with all his heart. In fact, David succeeded at what no one had been able to do before him. What was he able to accomplish?

> *The king and his men marched to Jerusalem to attack the*
> *Jebusites, who lived there. The Jebusites said to David,*
> *"You will not get in here."... Nevertheless, David captured the*
> *fortress of Zion, which is the City of David.*

> 2 Samuel 5:6–7

_____

_____

_____

What significance do you find in David being the one taking possession of the Promised Land?

_____

_____

_____

I wonder if there are any unconquered spiritual allotments fractured and fragmented in your life, like there have been in mine? What if the King is waiting to help His precious girl take possession of every spiritual blessing, to begin living a life that is profoundly effective as she loves Him back with all her heart, her mind, and every ounce of strength she can muster?

I wonder what that girl's prayer would look like?

_____

_____

_____

_____

_____

_____

_____

_____

ENDNOTES

1. Goodrick & Kohlenberger, *Zondervan NIV Exhaustive Concordance.*

2. University of Hertfordshire, "First concrete evidence that women are better multitaskers than men," ScienceDaily, July 19, 2010 (accessed May 5, 2013) http://www.sciencedaily.com/releases/2010/07/100719083042.htm Corrected

3. Goodrick & Kohlenberger, *Zondervan NIV Exhaustive Concordance.*

4. D. Martyn Lloyd-Jones, *The Christian Soldier: An Exposition of Ephesians 6:10–20* (Grand Rapids, Baker, 2003), 8:22.

5. Goodrick & Kohlenberger, *Zondervan NIV Exhaustive Concordance.*

6. Ibid.

7. Ibid.

8. Traylor, *Layman's Bible Book Commentary*, 41.

9. J. Hammond, *The Pulpit Commentary*, Vol. 5, 459.

10. Ibid., 460.

11. Goodrick & Kohlenberger, *Zondervan NIV Exhaustive Concordance.*

12. Ibid.

13. Ibid.

NOTES

LESSON 7

WHEN LOVE SATISFIES THE SOUL

O God, you are my God, earnestly I seek you; my soul thirsts
for you, my body longs for you, in a dry and weary land where
there is no water. I have seen you in the sanctuary and beheld
your power and your glory. Because your love is better than life,
my lips will glorify you. My soul will be satisfied as with the
richest of foods; with singing lips my mouth will praise you.

Psalm 63:1–4, NIV 1984

The transliteration of one of the Greek words for soul is psyche and refers to the immaterial (and eternal) part of the inner person, often meaning the animate self, which can be translated by pronouns: "my soul" = myself.[1]

The Hebrew word for soul means "breath"; by extension: life, life force, soul, an immaterial part of a person, the seat of emotion and desire; a creature or person as a whole.[2]

Psalm 63 expresses what it means to love God with all our souls. In verse 5, the Amplified Bible embraces the biblical definition for soul with "My whole being shall be satisfied." To love God with all your soul is to love Him with who you really are: not outward manifestations of love but love expressed through our emotions and our desires. Notice the wording David uses in this psalm: "earnest seeking," "thirsting souls," and physical "longing." The soul is what pulls everything together (heart, mind, and strength). Loving God with our souls is to love Him through our personalities—who we really are.

Only those who comprehend the King's love for and delight in them can love God with all their souls. Can you sense David's cravings? It's not a blind affection but a known commodity, for he says, "I have seen you in the sanctuary and beheld your power and your glory." David just wants more of what he knows and more still of what he has been given. God's love is precious to him. Here is a man who had every possession promised, yet we never hear David asking for more stuff. No, not for himself. No position, no property, no amount of money or fame could compare with the longings fulfilled in the depths of his soul by his God's richest love for him. This and only this was worth more than life itself.

I want that. Today, I would be satisfied with half this kind of longing. Sometimes I simply want to want a longing like David's. I want my soul to crave more and more of God: to long for, to thirst after, and to seek in earnest, the one who loves me with His whole being. I think you might too.

DAY 1

WE BEAR THE SIGNATURE OF OBEDIENCE

Your signature is unique. It's an identifiable mark separating you from everyone else. However, graphologists boast that elements of handwriting communicate trends in personalities. If analyzed, signatures can be very telling about who we really are, with striking accuracy. The same can be true of those who love God with all their souls. Each person's pursuit is unique, yet there are identifiable patterns that mark those who choose to follow God, holding nothing back. This week our study will be organized by various attributes that make up the signatures of those who love God with all their souls.

Last week we left the Israelites crossing the Jordan and learned the paramount importance of giving all our strength to take spiritual possession of whatever God speaks over our lives. Their story, as well as ours, continues in Judges.

Joshua distributed the land (as if he assigned it to the various tribes on paper), but many of the battles to take physical possession had not yet taken place. After the death of their leader, Joshua, the plight of God's people seemed hopeful. They rightly inquired (Judges 1:1) of the Lord who should be the first to take physical possession of their inheritance (or go to battle to conquer the land), and the Lord told them Judah was to go. We learn that Judah was successful, and so was the house of Joseph (vv. 22). Read verses 27–36 to learn what happened to the other six tribes and fill in the blanks. Do you see a pattern?

But _____did not _____ _____ the people of Beth Shan or Taanach or Dor or Ibleam or Megiddo and their surrounding settlements, . . .

Nor did _____ _____ _____ the Canaanites living in Gezer, . . .

Neither did _____ _____

_____ the Canaanites living in Kitron or Nahlol, so these Canaanites lived among them, . . .

Nor did_____ _____ _____ those living in Acco or Sidon or Ahlab or Aczib or Helbah or Aphek or Rehob,

Neither did _____ _____

_____ those living in Beth Shemesh or Beth Anath; . . .

The Amorites confined the _____ to the hill country, not allowing them to come down into the plain.

Not only did half of God's chosen people stop short of taking their inheritances, they gave themselves over to worshiping the gods of the Canaanites. *And God let them* (Judges 2:3). Then something even more devastating occurred:

> After that whole generation had been gathered to their ancestors, another generation grew up who knew neither the LORD nor what he had done for Israel.
>
> Judges 2:10

THE ISRAELITES' DISOBEDIENCE LED TO CERTAIN DEFEAT

The situation in Judges represents a sobering reality. Any of us can choose disobedience. We can shrink back from taking our inheritances. We can settle for less than God dreams for us. Settling allows us to be more accepting of sin and to mingle with the lesser things of evil. Oh, we might cry over it. We might regret our position, but no real change occurs. In time, before we know it, the dream of being the King's treasured posssession with the milk and honey experience gets buried somewhere deep within us, along with the memory of the God who covenanted to make Promised-Land living our reality. We move God from relevant and life-giving to relative and burdensome.

What were the Israelites supposed to do (Deuteronomy 4:9–10; 6:6–12)?

_____

_____

_____

Their problem began with slight disobedience, which resulted from familiar hindrances, and "because Israel had not zealously laid claim to the land as the Lord [had] directed, he withdrew his helping hand."[3]

Let this **NOT** be our story. Disobedience is the fast track of defeat in living the life our King desires for us. **Obedience**, rather, is the signature of those who love God with their whole beings, experiencing the fullest versions of the lives God planned for them.

CHRIST'S SIGNATURE OF OBEDIENCE LED TO ABSOLUTE VICTORY

Christ is the perfect example of the inseparable connection between love and obedience. Read how Jesus makes this connection clear in John 14:21–23. Explain the connection in your own words.

_____

_____

_____

Sometimes I need the obvious spelled out before my stubborn little eyes. If we really love Him, we will do what He says. _Period_. Richard Blackaby writes, "When we wrangle over doing what God says, that isn't an obedience problem but a love problem."[4]

Obedience is not a means of justification (Galatians 3:3). We cannot obey ourselves into heaven. Rather, it is the mark of loving Him with everything we are in light of everything He is and what He has done for us. We have the simplicity of the interwoven relationship of love and obedience from the horse's mouth.

HOW TO DEVELOP A SIGNATURE OF OBEDIENCE

What if you and I find ourselves in a slightly disobedient predicament? What if our souls currently reflect a propensity for stopping short of complete obedience? How do we grow in obedience so that our very personalities begin to reflect a love _for_ Him that comes through our obedience _to_ Him?

1. We Develop a Focused Life

> _Be very careful, then, how you live—not as unwise but as wise,_
> _making the most of every opportunity, because the days are evil._

Therefore do not be foolish, but understand
what the Lord's will is.

Ephesians 5:15–17

What three suggestions does Paul make in these verses?

1. Be

2. Make

3. Understand

My natural tendency is to waste hours on things having zero eternal significance. However, God has been teaching me that spending too much time on frivolous things I enjoy is unwise. It's not being careful, making the most of every opportunity. It is squandering the resources God has entrusted to me. He has been moving me from using time foolishly to understanding what His will is in this area. As a result, I am becoming much more focused and intentional about my time.

Understanding the Lord's will takes time. Discerning which choices are foolish and which are not requires an ability to listen and hear the Holy Spirit. Can you identify one way Paul's instructions can help you move toward living a more focused life? What will you do?

_____

_____

_____

2. We Develop a Disciplined Life

What does Paul encourage Timothy to do in 1 Timothy 4:7?

_____

We studied aspects of developing physical strength last week. Today, think about your spiritual "body." Is there an area that needs attention? Do you need to discipline yourself to acquire a habit of solitude (without your phone or computer), to practice thankfulness and gratitude, or to get out of bed earlier?

None of us were born disciplined people. We develop discipline through practice. What you and I know (yet hold vehement disdain for) is that *discipline breeds discipline*. And the opposite is also true. The less disciplined we are in one area, the less disciplined we become in others.

What does Paul warn Timothy about in 2 Timothy 3:5-6?

_____

The Amplified Bible calls these women *"silly and weak-natured and spiritually dwarfed women."* This is not the kind of women we should aspire to become. Be assured, *not* actively developing habits that lead to godliness will lead to spiritually stunted growth.

"Spiritual maturity comes not from learning secrets and
gaining insider information about God's kingdom,
but from walking faithfully with God and regularly obeying
what He tells you."[5]

Lord, help us! We should be closer to godliness than we are. We want to be obedient to you, but we are so spiritually weak. You are our only hope. Show us where to begin choosing you over mere pleasures and enjoyments. Help us endure the hard work of establishing new habits that lead to godliness.

3. We Develop a Listening Life

Read Matthew 17:5. The meaning of the Greek word for *listen* is similar to our use of *listen* when we fully expect action to follow the listening.[6] When I say "Listen to me," what I am really conveying is "Stop. Look at Mom. I am about to tell you to do something, and I expect you to do it." What does Psalm 81:8–10 tell us God will do when we listen to Him?

_____

_____

_____

I agree with Richard Blackaby in his book *Unlimiting God*: "If God has more to say to me, I want to hear it."[7] We listen to God primarily through Scripture. The more we listen, the better we learn to distinguish His voice. Recognizing His voice is how we follow more closely. "When there's a limit to what we hear from God, it's a limit we have chosen for ourselves."[8]

> *The gatekeeper opens the gate for him, and the sheep listen to his voice. He calls his own sheep by name and leads them out. When he has brought out all his own, he goes on ahead of them, and his sheep follow him because they know his voice.*
>
> John 10:3–4

> *"The Bible is not an end in itself, but a means to bring men to an intimate and satisfying knowledge of God, that they may enter into Him, that they may delight in His Presence, and may taste and know the inner sweetness of the very God Himself in the core and center of their hearts."*[9]
>
> A. W. Tozer

WE DEVELOP A TRUSTING LIFE

Read Hebrews 11:1–6. Use your last moments of study today to think diligently about the concepts presented. Begin to trace in your mind the relationship that intertwines love for God, faith, and obedience. If you were to draw a picture, what might this relationship look like? If you need help, read the examples given in Hebrews 11. Use this space to illustrate or describe your understanding:

Close your time today in prayer.

Lord, I want to live a life that longs for you alone. Sometimes I don't know where to start. Give me eyes to see how to become the woman you dreamed me to be. Please don't give up on me. Keep nudging me when I cannot see your hand. Keep teaching me to follow in complete obedience when I would rather settle for just some of your will. Make me thirsty for more of your love until my lips are parched, my skin is dry, and my soul desires your love more than life.

DAY 2

WE BEAR THE SIGNATURE OF LOVE

Our first adoption resulted from a casual statement in a history class. There I learned about the one-child policy China adopted in 1979 and the plight of countless girls raised in orphanages. At the age of fourteen, they are cast out of these orphanages, destitute, often used as prostitutes, and with one of the highest suicide rates in the world. From that moment, God placed a burning desire in me to adopt one of those girls. I was nineteen.

As God would have it, fifteen years later, my husband and I traveled to China with our two daughters to pick up a perfectly healthy baby girl. We traveled with other families, uniting with Chinese children who were, well, *not* so perfect. Some children were simply over the age of six. Others had issues, some life threatening. Ally, a vibrant six-year-old, took our breath away, and two years later we found ourselves back on a bus, headed for our own *not-so-perfect* young lady.

Unlike our previous adoption, as we signed documents, the authorities rattled off a list of things our new daughter could not do and made us stamp our thumbs in red ink to signify that we understood her imperfections. "You understand she can't . . . She will not be able to . . ." and so on. Adding to the humiliation, they asked us in her presence (in Chinese) if we still wanted her. Shocked and appalled, Chad and I responded with an emphatic "Yes!"

What a way to begin. At first I was indignant. Then I was petrified, thinking, *This is not what I signed up for, Lord. What are you doing to our perfect family?* Finally, I found myself in a puddle of tears before Him in our hotel room, where He used the experience to teach me something about Himself.

God sees us in a situation where we will surely die unless someone intervenes. Forced to live a life of abuse and treated like property, people like you and me are then discarded. Despairing of life, they end it and spend eternity in hell. But He can do something about this atrocity.

He comes down to get us. He pays the exorbitant price (1 John 4:10). He brings you and me into His family. Then the accuser comes forward (Revelation 12:10). It's my turn. Satan invades my personal space with disapproval in his breath.

"Are you aware she . . . She is worthless! . . . Don't waste the effort. You know she will never love You," calls the enemy. His taunts continue, the pursuer unmoved.

"Yes, I know," responds the Father at each and every accusation.

When he is finished, the enemy vehemently asks, "Do you still want her?"

Without hesitation—because of Christ God replies with a resounding "*YES.*"

When it's your turn, the accusations are a little different, but He indeed wants you too, in spite of your imperfections. We both have a new family and a new life!

God makes His home in you and me (John 14:23), gives us more than we could ask for (Ephesians 1), and time proves the enemy correct (Romans 3:23). You and I are all those awful things. But God loves us anyway (John 3:16). Still, I am prone to lie and steal and bent on personal destruction, and so are you. We work against Him. Even though He loves us with perfect love, we look elsewhere for it and settle for imitations. We squander the new life we were given.

I say, "What a waste! Why the heartache, Lord? Why put yourself through all the drama—why take the risk? Why pour yourself into someone who cannot return the affection and instead gives it freely to others? The enemy benefits from your sacrifice."

"Even in your worst state," He confidently and compassionately confides, "you are worth my pursuit."

Write out Romans 5:8.

_____

_____

_____

THE RESULTS OF HIS LOVE

What else can we do but love Him back? And in the course of loving Him, a love for others is cultivated and grows. We begin to mourn the plight of the orphan. New shoes become less of a need than giving money for a village to build a water well. The neighbor's reckless and irresponsible behavior that once irritated now saddens us. Over time, loving Him back, to those around us, looks a lot like loving our neighbor.

Love for others is the signature of one who loves God with all her soul. It is a directive, like obedience, that results because of His love for us:

> Dear friends, since God so loved us, we also ought to love one another. No one has ever seen God; but if we love one another, God lives in us and his love is made complete in us.
>
> 1 John 4:11–12

My daughter Addison loves games. One of her favorites is Life.® Every player selects a car and a pink or blue game piece to maneuver through the challenges faced across the board. Winning is simple: finish with the most money. When the road forks and career paths must be chosen, astute players choose the path that leads to the highest-paying salaries. Players who choose the path of lower-paying jobs, well . . . lose. In essence, this choice is simple: choose the path that leads to winning the game.

In 1 Corinthians 9:24, although Paul is writing about our spiritual pursuits, he uses a common metaphor to which we can relate:

> Run in such a way as to get the prize.

In essence, Paul is saying, "Choose the path that leads to winning." Today, imagine two paths: one leading to loving God with all our souls, the other leading to a life that loves in part. We are familiar with the path of halfhearted pursuit. Today, let's choose the path to obtain the **signature of love** and run our spiritual races to win lasting crowns.

THE PATH OF LOVE

On this road are indicators of a life moving toward loving others based upon Scripture. Read each indicator and the corresponding verses. Then write how the verses relate to the statement above. This is a time for God's Word to speak to you without my interference. Pick a color for your car and a pink game piece. Let the game begin!

Clean Out the Car before You Start

Romans 12:9; 1 Peter 1:22

_____

_____

_____

Determine Your Destination

John 13:34–35; Ephesians 5:1–2

_____

_____

_____

Set your GPS to the following destination: To _____ a life of _____(Ephesians 5:2).

Understand What Fuels the Journey

2 Corinthians 5:18–19

_____

_____

_____

Consider Other Drivers

Philippians 2:3–4

> *Do nothing out of selfish ambition or vain conceit. Rather, in humility value others above yourselves, not looking to your own interests but each of you to the interests of others.*

_____

_____

_____

Be Sure You Know How to Operate the Vehicle

1 Corinthians 13:1–8. I encourage you to write out these verses.

_____

_____

_____

_____

_____

_____

_____

Make Frequent Stops to Exercise Your Learning

Luke 10:30–37

_____

_____

_____

Keep Going Straight

Proverbs 4:25

_____

_____

_____

Rough Road Ahead: Wear Your Seat Belt

Luke 6:27

_____

_____

_____

Grow on the Journey

Philippians 1:9; 1 Thessalonians 3:12

_____

_____

_____

Encourage Others on the Road

Hebrews 10:24

> *And let us consider how we may spur one another on*
> *toward love and good deeds.*

_____

_____

The **path of love** is the only path to win the race marked out for us. We need to know what it looks like, learn how to navigate it, and choose this path every time. And when our attitudes, actions, and mouths take a detour, we need to return in humble repentance at the first opportunity.

DAY 3

WE BEAR THE SIGNATURE OF PASSION

Complacency is a deadly foe of all spiritual growth. Acute desire must be present or there will be no manifestation of Christ to His people. He waits to be wanted.[10]

> *As the deer pants for streams of water,*
> *so my soul pants for you, O God.*

Psalm 42:1

Yes, the King waits for you. He holds His plans for you in His hands. He tenderly speaks to you, but He will not push you out of complacency. Your God, the lover of your soul, waits for you to want Him.

We will not find our souls panting feverishly for anything other than ourselves in a rushed fifteen-minute "quiet time," in a frantic completion of our group studies, or in a prayer life consisting of our own concerns and the concerns of the ones we cherish. The glorious enlightenment experienced by those whose souls pant for God (the kind that illuminated the very face of Moses) resulted from the discovery that God does not have to conform to our fractured understandings resulting from our limited engagement.

> *My heart says of you, "Seek his face!" Your face, LORD, I will seek*

Psalm 27:8

In the movie *Galaxy Quest*, Tim Allen plays an actor in a TV series mimicking our *Star Trek*. Allen portrays a character similar to Captain Kirk. The movie opens with Allen and his co-stars attending a Galaxy Quest convention crowded with people dressed in costumes associated with the series. Allen meets an attendee in space garb who asks for his help. Allen misinterprets the request as a public-speaking gig and agrees to go. He finds himself in outer space on a spaceship identical to the one he pretends to navigate, fighting alien enemies. When he returns to earth, he hysterically reports to his undaunted crew, "It's real! It's all real!"

At some point in time, those whose souls panted feverishly after God came to this conclusion: He's really real! And there is nothing on this planet that can compare to the thrill of Him. Their lives began to take on a dimension I can only describe as spiritually derived **passion.**

The signature of those who leave lives of complacency in exchange for the lives God dreams them to live is **passion**. Intensity, fervent devotion, inexplicable joy, and exponential spiritual growth, even amid adversity, exude from a passionate follower of Christ. Investigating the lives of passionate God-lovers, we will see this quality spill out across the pages of Scripture. When we finish today's lesson, you will be able to recognize passion when you see it and know how it develops in the woman seeking to love God with all her soul.

PASSION IS A GAME-CHANGING, GOD-DRIVING FORCE

Read Nehemiah 1:1–10; 2:1–5. What information is given that might suggest this man is a passionate pursuer of God?

_____

_____

_____

Now read Acts 9:1–8. Both Nehemiah and Paul accomplished greatness for the kingdom. Their compulsion came from within. One simply possessed an acute awareness of God and His promises for His people. The other experienced a face-to-face encounter with Jesus. Both allowed God to change the direction of their lives, putting aside previous expectations and dreams to pursue something bigger than themselves. We see this in Paul's writing:

> *Though I am free and belong to no one, I have made myself a*
> *slave to everyone, to win as many as possible.*
>
> 1 Corinthians 9:19

Spiritual encounters with Jesus continue to have the same game-changing effect on people today.

PASSION REQUIRES AN INTENSE FOCUS

In 1 Corinthians 9:24–27, what does Paul suggest loving God with our lives should look like?

_____

_____

_____

PASSION LOOKS OUT OF PLACE

We find passion acceptable in certain arenas. We never question the time and money spent supporting favorite sports teams. Guys with painted bodies attending these events are praised for their enthusiasm. Hundreds of thousands of people frequent countless games, spend millions to sport their colors, and adorn their homes with team paraphernalia. I know someone who plans to play his team's anthem at his funeral! But we don't find that *weird* or a little *too passionate.* Adopting six kids—now that's too much for people to handle. *It looks out of place.*

How does passion look out of place in the following verses?

1 Samuel 17:32–33

_____

_____

Mark 3:7–21

_____

_____

_____

Acts 9:26–29

_____

_____

_____

> *Never be lacking in zeal, but keep your spiritual fervor,*
> *serving the Lord.*
>
> Romans 12:11

PASSION BRINGS OUT THE UGLY IN PEOPLE

Describe the ugliness demonstrated in the following examples:

Nehemiah 6:1–9

_____

_____

_____

Mark 3:22–27

_____

_____

_____

2 Corinthians 10:1–2

_____

_____

_____

Can you recall a time when ugliness was the response to someone's passionate pursuit of God? How did that person handle the situation?

_____

_____

_____

What is the best way to respond to the ugliness displayed in these kinds of situations?

_____

_____

_____

PASSION HELPS ACCOMPLISH KINGDOM BUSINESS

Nehemiah orchestrated the rebuilding of the walls in Jerusalem (Nehemiah 7:1–4) as well as organized the city to be successfully resettled (7:73); he also brought the people together to enter into a binding agreement to follow God (9:38). Had he sat back, complacent with his cup-bearing responsibilities, he would have forfeited his participation in God's eternal purposes.

> *At Iconium Paul and Barnabas went as usual into the Jewish synagogue. There they spoke so effectively that a great number of Jews and Gentiles believed.*

> Acts 14:1

Paul spent the rest of his days speaking and writing effectively for the kingdom. And we, along with countless others, are the benefactors of his passionate pursuit to live a life that loved the one who loved him first.

HOW DO WE ATTAIN THIS KIND OF PASSION?

Regardless of personality or propensities, you too are a candidate for God-exalting passionate pursuit of your Savior. Such fervor is not limited those graced with sanguine optimism or charismatic leadership abilities. This kind of passion is attainable for anyone willing to pursue the Pursuer.

1. Recognize Passion Is Spiritually Given, Not Externally Driven

We cannot conjure up a passion for Christ that brings anything but exhaustion. God gives the passion, if we will but listen to receive it and respond to live it out.

It's important to note that passion does not equal sensationalism. Passion is not displayed only in what we might think of as emotion-driven behaviors and exciting endeavors. Consider Leviticus 14:54–57. This passage is no less divinely inspired than Exodus 33:18, *"Now show me your glory."* Passion does not equal perpetual exhilaration. Not every moment in Christ is a show-me-your-glory kind of experience. Sometimes the passion-driven life is about mildew and bright spots.

2. Pursue the Source

In His restorative encounter with Peter, Jesus offered one last emphatic word of instruction:

> *Then he said to him, "Follow me!"*
>
> John 21:19

Again, we will not attain the passion contained in the pages of Scripture in flighty moments with five-minute devotionals and giving Him our leftovers. Real passion will emerge when we decide He is who we want beyond all other passions. The God-given passion of world-changing kingdom builders is possessed when we begin to make Him wait for us no longer.

3. Find Passionate Friends

Find passionate Christians and do what they do. Look how Paul encourages the Corinthians:

> *Follow my example, as I follow the example of Christ.*
>
> 1 Corinthians 11:1

Have you heard the advice for healthy eating habits that suggests finding a skinny friend and eating like her? That is similar to what Paul is suggesting. Paul is not placing himself on the same plane as Jesus, nor is he telling us to become carbon copies of him. Paul is offering his life as a flesh-and-blood example of someone pursuing the Lord and Savior. Notice, he inherently gave the Corinthians permission to deviate if he ceased to follow the example of Christ.

If you do not know any passionate pursuers personally, the world is at your fingertips, so find some! Some of my closest mentors in the faith are people I have never met this side of a screen, or they lived a hundred years before me. Read books. Study the lives of the faithful who walked before our day. God will provide the examples necessary for moving you from complacency to becoming a panting pursuer of the King.

Make Him wait to be wanted no longer. What should your prayer look like today?

_____

_____

_____

_____

_____

_____

_____

_____

Day 4

We Bear the Signature of Radiance

The house we purchased a few years ago came with several outside amenities, most of which were broken. We spent money hand over fist just to get the pool working. Attached was a pool house with a broken bathroom toilet, hot tub, and sauna and a leaking roof. Honestly, the experts recommended the whole building be torn down. Tree roots came through the hot tub, and mice made the sauna their home. It was a disaster. But when we decided to adopt four more children, it became clear I would not be able to find a single quiet moment to write *inside* the house. We suddenly found potential in our dilapidated, mice-infested pool house.

We filled the hot tub with concrete, installed carpet, and had the roof repaired, the bathroom fixtures replaced, and the mice exterminated. We hung new doors, painted the walls, and added curtains, and I moved my office files and books "outside" to a perfect environment for writing. What was once worthy of total destruction has been transformed into a sanctuary for furthering the kingdom.

My pool-house-to-office transformation is a picture of what happens when you and I choose to let go of the shame we once bore to be transformed into the women God dreams us to become. The unsightly and discarded are given new life and new purpose.

Read Psalm 34:2–8. Write out verse 5.

_____

_____

The Hebrew word for *radiance* means "to beam with joy."[11] Maybe this is why we relate radiance to an expectant mother. The outward appearance is telling of an inward condition. In the same way, the joy of Christians is a response to God's relentless love and cogent power in our lives. The prominent place He holds within shines through our outward expressions. **Radiance** in the life of a Christian is the signature of one who loves God with all of her soul.

"The truest joy springs out of love."[12]

RADIANCE IN THE OLD TESTAMENT

To catch a glimpse of what radiance looks like, we first turn to the Old Testament. Read Deuteronomy 16:1–14. This chapter describes the requirements of the three feasts the Israelites were to celebrate each year before the Lord. Two of them concern our topic today: the Feast of Weeks (vv. 9–12), and the Feast of Tabernacles (vv. 13–14). What requirement did these feasts have in common?

_____

_____

How worshiping God differed from the pagan religions of the Canaanites! Far from rejoicing, other religions required mutilations of flesh, human blood spilled over altars, and children made to walk through fire, or worse. What a contrast God showed the Israelites! How much greater it is to worship Him alone!

Now read Psalm 4:6–7:

> *Many are asking, "Who can show us any good?" Let the light of your face shine upon us, O LORD. You have filled my heart with greater joy than when their grain and new wine abound.*

What do you think David wants to communicate about God in these verses?

_____

_____

Read Psalm 43:3–4. How does David refer to God in these verses?

_____

_____

RADIANCE IN THE NEW TESTAMENT

Bringing animal sacrifices and offerings to the Lord to rejoice before Him a couple of times a year is not our practice this side of the Old Testament. What does the New Testament have to say about joy? Read each verse and record how joy relates to the Christian life.

Romans 12:12

_____

_____

Philippians 3:1

_____

_____

1 Thessalonians 5:16

_____

_____

We also learn in John 15:9–11 that our joy comes from Christ. Jesus not only wants us to have His joy and His delight, He wants us to enjoy Him in the highest sense and in the fullest measure.[13] Record what these verses tell us about how we attain His joy:

> *You became imitators of us and of the Lord, for you welcomed the message in the midst of severe suffering with the joy given by the Holy Spirit.*
>
> 1 Thessalonians 1:6

*Though you have not seen him, you love him; and even though
you do not see him now, you believe in him and are filled with
an inexpressible and glorious joy, for you are receiving the end
result of your faith, the salvation of your souls.*

1 Peter 1:8–9

_____

_____

_____

_____

So far, joy seems to be a win-win. From the Old Testament to the New, God commands us to be joyful. He promises to fill us with His personal joy until it overflows within us as we seek to be loved by Him. Psalm 37:4 tells us that if we will delight in Him, God will give us the desires of our heart. This is a really good gig! Why then are Christians not more joyful?

*Take Delight in the Lord, and he will give you the desires of
your heart.*

Psalm 37:4

WHERE IS THE JOY?

Joy must be fought for and won. The enemy is out to steal our joy, and we are handing it over without a fight. Paul asked the Galatians a penetrating question:

What has happened to all your joy?

Galatians 4:15, NIV 1984

Sometimes joy is lost due to the frantic pace of life and the burdens that accompany our ridiculous schedules. Other times there is an encroaching sense of discouragement or even doom about a situation. Sin will always pull us away from experiencing the fullness of God. Sometimes we find ourselves in an unhappy state we cannot move beyond, thinking emotion defines our joy—not understanding that our radiance is just the result of being satisfied and even thrilled with our God.

What happens to all *your* joy?

_____

_____

_____

_____

_____

Whatever you have written above, we can stand together to fight for our joy.

HOW DO WE FIGHT TO BECOME MORE RADIANT?

There are obvious and important avenues, such as choosing to remain in His love (John 15:9–11), rejecting joy-stealing thoughts and actions, and guarding our lives against sin. We need to be mindful of these in our fight to become more radiant. There also are two other themes that developed in my studies specifically related to our fight for joy.

1. Choose to Rejoice

Paul's letter to the Philippians has joy as its central theme. A renowned summary is "I rejoice; rejoice ye."[14] Paul uses the word *joy* or a variant eighteen times. Mesmerizing even the most love-stricken follower of Christ is the realization that Paul wrote such a luminous letter during a time when the present was dismal and his future looked darkest. Chained to a guard, isolated, and imprisoned indefinitely, Paul continued to live out his calling through surest pain and suffering, giving his life so others would know this Love spilling out of him until his dying breath.

How is Paul joyful during this season of life? Is he just a super-Christian, or can he teach us about loving God with all *our* souls? Read Philippians 1:3–8. Why do you think Paul could pray with joy amid his circumstances?

_____

_____

_____

Read the following verses, and write in your own words why Paul found reason to rejoice:

Philippians 1:12–18

_____

_____

_____

Philippians 1:21–26

_____

_____

_____

2. Be Productive

Compare Philippians 2:1–2 with Deuteronomy 16:14–15 and record any similarities. Why do you think Paul uses the same words? How can the Philippians affect his joy?

> *Be joyful at your Feast. . . . For the* Lord *your God will bless you*
> *in all your harvest and in all the work of your hands,*
> *and your joy will be complete.*
>
> Deuteronomy 16:14–15

_____

_____

_____

Deuteronomy speaks of God's promise of abundant productivity of the land when His people walked in obedience. God promised to give them reason to be joyful. They would be able to look around and see His goodness to them, so tremendous that their joy would overflow. Paul draws from this idea in communicating to the Philippians that when they grow in love, in spirit, and in purpose, his joy will be fulfilled.

Read the following verses and record what brought each person joy:

John 3:27–29. Why was John the Baptist joyful?

_____

_____

_____

Romans 16:19; 2 Corinthians 7:4. Why was Paul joyful?

_____

_____

_____

3 John 1:4. Why was John joyful?

_____

_____

_____

A pattern should emerge. Our joy increases as we live out God's call on our lives.[15] What joy brings people in the New Testament and beyond is exactly what it brought in the Old Testament in relationship to productivity. Could it be the lack of radiance throughout the Christian community is the result of too many living spiritually unproductive lives—accepting the Christian mediocrity that never moves mountains or brings lost people into eternal blessing? Let it not be so in us! Instead, may we embrace our callings and choose joy in any circumstance:

> *Let us fix our eyes on Jesus, the author and perfecter of our faith, who for the joy set before him endured the cross, scorning its shame, and sat down at the right hand of the throne of God.*
>
> Hebrews 12:2, NIV 1984

When delight spills out of our lives from a love relationship with our God, it will not depend on how much we have to do or the urgent problems upon us. Our desires will not simply be the latest cars or a health-and-wealth gospel. Our delight will reflect the greater good of others and our involvement in it. We will be joy choosers and joyful producers—doing whatever God has called us to do. We will rejoice as we go, no matter the circumstances.

"For the joy set before us," we will

take captive our selfish thoughts for Him . . .

take that next step of faith for Him . . .

take tremendous courage from Him . . .

do the hard thing for Him . . .

endure sickness or disease for Him . . .

serve our lives to death for Him . . .

give until it hurts for Him . . .

let go of our dreams for Him . . .

leave our homes and go . . . for Him.

In the words of John Piper, *"Nothing shows the direction of the deep winds of the soul like the demand for radical, sin-destroying, Christ-exalting joy in God."*[16]

DAY 5

WE BEAR THE SIGNATURE OF HOPE

Let us hold unswervingly to the hope we profess,
for he who promised is faithful.

Hebrews 10:23

For several weeks at least, and possibly for years, God has been calling out, longing to embrace you and me with His love. We are His treasured possession. We are the King's delight. He has waited for us to be in just this place. *And we have shown up.*

I wonder if anybody keeps showing up because you are longing for answers to some difficult questions. Life is messy. People get sick. Jobs are lost. Economies fail, stealing our means of support. Natural disasters strike. Some situations are just not going to get better. Injustices around us prevail, some hitting closer to home than we would like.

As I write today, yet another national atrocity has left numerous young and innocent dead, injuring dozens of others. We find ourselves asking why. Why does a just God not act? How can a God who cannot look on evil allow such violence, letting the guilty go unpunished and the innocent pay with their lives?

In today's lesson, He speaks to us through an obscure prophet addressing a common dilemma. In three short chapters, Habakkuk encapsulates what it looks like to love God completely, in the midst of trouble, suffering, and responsibility, bearing the signature of one who faces the darker realities of life: **hope.**

My favorite book of the Bible, hands down, is Habakkuk. There is no better place to land our investigation of what it looks like to love God with our whole beings than from one whose name means "to embrace" or "to be embraced."[17] Habakkuk understands. Today *we will* find hope in the midst of trouble, suffering, and too much responsibility.

HABAKKUK ASKED A BIG QUESTION

Read Habakkuk 1:1–4. What big question did Habakkuk ask God?

_____

_____

Did he feel like God was not there or did not see? Or saw but didn't care? We get the sense that the prophet had been praying without receiving an answer. The violence, injustice, and conflict continued. Habakkuk experienced his own version of my Gazebo Time. He was in a difficult place, spiritually and emotionally.

Friend, it is possible to get to the end of Week 7 in a bad place spiritually and emotionally. Like Habakkuk, we can find the burden and the pain can be unbearable when the big questions of life go unanswered. Look further. Hope is coming.

Read verse 5. How did God respond?

_____

_____

At this point, I can imagine Habakkuk moving toward the edge of his seat, rubbing his hands together, thinking, *Now THAT'S what I'm talking about! Here it comes! God is about to do some righteous smitation around here! He's going to get the attention of those sinful, unrighteous, conniving, backsliding Jews—so they will come to their senses, and turn their hearts back to Him. We can be a great nation again!*—until God continued.

Read verses 6–11. God confided in Habakkuk about His great idea. What was His idea for bringing justice to the injustices in Habakkuk's world?

_____

_____

Read verses 12–17. Habakkuk once again questioned God. He acknowledged discipline was deserved, but based upon God's character of holiness, how could He look on and not act? How was that a good solution? The horrible Babylonians were worse than the unfaithful Jews!

Have you ever been in a situation like Habakkuk's, where the answer you expected did not come? Instead you received a difficult word—one that seemed less than just or fair—an answer you did not want? You seemed to say, like our prophet, "Are you sure, Lord?" Describe your experience.

_____

_____

_____

Habakkuk interrupted the dialogue between himself and the Lord to speak as the narrator, directed to the reader:

> *I will stand at my watch and station myself on the ramparts;*
> *I will look to see what he will say to me, and what answer I am*
> *to give to this complaint.*

Habakkuk 2:1

We do not know how long Habakkuk waited, but God responded with a word that should ring familiar in your ears. Read Habakkuk 2:2–20.

Habakkuk was charged with writing down the vision and making it plain enough that it could be delivered to and understood by everyone. Be assured, the bulk of the vision speaks of the justice awaiting the Babylonians for the horrible things they were going to do to God's people (vv. 6–20). In five woes, God communicated He is, indeed, a God of justice. The bad guys could work to bring discipline to His people, but they would pay for their heinous violence. History tells us the Babylonians were, indeed, overtaken by the Persians within a generation. Justice came.

Fill in the blanks with the last part of verse 4:

> but the _____ _____ will _____
> by his _____.

God communicated that there was and would remain a contrast between the righteous and the unrighteous. Nothing had changed. He is who He says He is. He can do what He says He can do. Habakkuk's job was to trust God's unseen word *as if it had already been accomplished.*

How in the world can we find hope in the midst of suffering, overwhelming responsibilities, and problems without solutions? We learn from these verses that God *is* in control of the hard situations. He redeems our difficult times and hopeless places.

FINDING HOPE

Pull your Bible in close. You are going to read out loud. If you have access to music you find inspirational (CDs, Christian radio stations, iTunes, or Pandora), get ready to play it. Read Habakkuk 3:1 AMP below, and you will see why:

> *A prayer of Habakkuk the prophet, set to wild, enthusiastic,*
> *and triumphal music.*

Cue some wild, enthusiastic, and triumphal music. Prepare to read Habakkuk's prayer out loud.

Begin with Habakkuk 3:2. Pray it back to the Lord. Do it more than once if you need. We can always ask Him to be huge in ways we can understand Him. And when we need correction or chastisement, we can beg for mercy in the midst of His wrath.

Read verses 3–15 silently or aloud. At this point in the prayer, the prophet tells of a vision of God: holy, awesome, and mighty. Then he recounts some of His wonders he has only heard about, as if he were there as they happened.

Now read verses 16–18 aloud.

How can Habakkuk pray such a prayer? Nothing has changed. His circumstances are the same. Things are really bad, and they are going to get much worse. How can he rejoice in the midst of unprecedented badness?

I think I know . . .

Read Habakkuk's concluding verse, 3:19:

> *The Lord God is my Strength, my personal bravery, and my*
> *invincible army; He makes my feet like hinds' feet and will*
> *make me to walk [not to stand still in terror, but to walk] and*
> *make [spiritual] progress upon my high places [of trouble,*
> *suffering, or responsibility]!* (AMP).

Somehow Habakkuk took courage from his experiences with God and His rich understanding of His character. He *knew* God was listening and that *He was* in control. Habakkuk understood that the climax to this eternal story is incredible. *It is victorious!* And it is a page-turner. He accepted the difficult reality that his job was to continue to live by faith . . . no matter what.

Habakkuk did not come to this place of complete abandonment of self to God overnight. In this one prayer, a lifetime of walking with God, learning to love Him, and maturing in godliness resounds. It is a beautiful signature of a sojourner who loves God with his whole being.

Today, if you have any kind of big question, take it to Him. Ask Him. He delights in *you.*

Look for His response and wait. Keep watching until you receive a response. If the response is hard to accept, ask Him to reveal himself more to you.

Ask Him to help you see Him in your struggle and what He is trying to accomplish in your life. Ask Him to renew His mighty works in your life in a way you can understand, to make himself real to you.

When you don't see anything, take courage to believe in what is unseen as if you *could* see it (Habakkuk 3:17). Commit to this kind of faith.

When you fall or you get discouraged, get right back up and continue to trust Him. You are not a failure because you fall down once in a while.

Declare your intentions. Read Habakkuk 3:19 aloud as a declaration. *Your God* is your Strength. He is *your* personal bravery. He is *your* invincible army. You *will NOT* stand still in terror. You *will* walk. You *will* make spiritual progress in the midst of trouble, suffering, and too much responsibility. The enemy has no hold on you. You *will* rejoice in what you cannot see. You *will*. You **will**.

Nothing short of wild, enthusiastic, and triumphal music could accompany such a powerful signature of hope!

> *Lord Jesus, today we choose to believe you, even when we can't see you working—even when what we believe you have said to us has not come to fruition. We REFUSE to stand still. We REFUSE to be stopped in our spiritual tracks. Help us find strength in you until our faith becomes reality!*

ENDNOTES

1. Goodrick & Kohlenberger, *Zondervan NIV Exhaustive Concordance.*

2. Ibid.

3. Note on Judges 2:1–5, *Zondervan NIV Study Bible,* (Grand Rapids: Zondervan, 2002), 332.

4. Blackaby, *Unlimiting God,* 92.

5. Ibid., 36.

6. Goodrick & Kohlenberger, *Zondervan NIV Exhaustive Concordance.*

7. Blackaby, *Unlimiting God,* 41.

8. Ibid., 46.

9. Tozer, *The Pursuit of God,* 10.

10. Ibid., 17.

11. Goodrick & Kohlenberger, *Zondervan NIV Exhaustive Concordance.*

12. B. C. Caffin, *The Pulpit Commentary,* H. D. M. Spence, Joseph S. Exell, eds., (Grand Rapids: Wm. B. Eerdmans, 1962), 20:65.

13. B. Thomas, *The Pulpit Commentary,* H. D. M. Spence, Joseph S. Exell, eds., (Grand Rapids: Wm. B. Eerdmans Publishing, 1958), 17:292.

14. R. Finlayson, *The Pulpit Commentary,* H. D. M. Spence, Joseph S. Exell, eds., (Grand Rapids: Wm. B. Eerdmans, 1958), 17:27.

15. Thomas, *The Pulpit Commentary,* 281.

16. John Piper, *When I Don't Desire God: How to Fight for Joy* (Wheaton: Crossway, 2004), 31.

17. W. J. Deane, *The Pulpit Commentary,* H. D. M. Spence, Joseph S. Exell, eds., (Grand Rapids: Wm. B. Eerdmans, 1963), 14:iii.

NOTES

LESSON 8

WHEN LIFE OVERFLOWS

And therefore the Lord [earnestly] waits [expecting, looking, and longing] to be gracious to you; and therefore He lifts
Himself up, that He may have mercy on you and show loving-
kindness to you. For the Lord is a God of justice. Blessed (happy,
fortunate, to be envied) are all those who [earnestly] wait for
Him, who expect and look and long for Him [for His victory,
His favor, His love, His peace, His joy, and His matchless,
unbroken companionship]!

Isaiah 30:18, AMP

What if you and I made the King wait for us no longer? What would happen if we longed for Him in return for His expecting, looking, and longing for us? In the opening pages of our journey together, I asked the question, "What if there is a connection between the love-initiating and love-enabling Father and the life-giving Son?"

I came that they may have and enjoy life,
and have it in abundance (to the full, till it overflows.

John 10:10, AMP

Could it be that responding to His love, by living out the Greatest Commandment (God's requirement that we love Him back), is the catalyst for experiencing the abundant, full, and overflowing life Christ came to give?

When you choose to make Him wait no longer, He promises your life will overflow. This is the *very reason* He came. Did you notice what He did not promise? Jesus did **NOT** come to give us mediocrity. He did **NOT** come to give us lives spent fulfilling selfish and meaningless agendas and choosing to wallow in our puddles of contentment, splashing in familiarity and selective love. He did **NOT** come to bring us guilt, wounded hearts that won't heal, despair, or years of unproductive service.

No, He came to give you a life that stretches beyond ordinary. He stands in heaven look-ing for **ANYTHING** that could bring opportunity to be loving and gracious to you. His mercy and kindness are specific—meeting you in your particular need and blessing you in ways only you and He are privileged to share. Make no mistake: there is more for you when you choose to participate wholeheartedly rather than loving Him in part and settling for mediocrity. He came to give you a full life out of His own fullness:

> *For out of His fullness (abundance) we have all received [all had a share and we were all supplied with] one grace after another and spiritual blessing upon spiritual blessing and even favor upon favor and gift [heaped] upon gift.*

John 1:16, AMP

What exactly do we receive through His fullness? What can you expect in a life that overflows, with spiritual blessing piled upon spiritual blessing, favor upon favor, and gifts heaped upon more gifts? Keep reading. He wants you to know. And if my excitement is any indication of His antsy anticipation for you, oh, sweet sister, **this is going to be good!**

DAY 1

HE LISTENS TO YOU

Which would you prefer: eating dinner at a restaurant plastered with flat-screen TVs and loud, conversation-squelching music, or dining with background mood music in an environment that encourages dialogue among dinner guests? Regardless of age or the volume level you keep the radio in your car, I'm sure I can guess your preference. Although we race through our days at lightning speed, dividing our attention across five or six tasks we attempt simultaneously, most of us crave *undivided* attention. Particularly in our close, intimate relationships, we prefer our message fall on listening ears. We want to be heard and understood. One of the benefits of living out the Greatest Commandment, experiencing life as Jesus intends, is God's attentiveness to our prayers. He leans over out of heaven to listen to you.

EXAMPLES OF GOD'S ATTENTIVENESS

How can I be certain His ear is bent toward those His loves? Simply, put, He tells us, specifically, through His word (John 9:31; 1 Peter 3:12; 1 John 3:22). We can also hone in on God's attentiveness if we tune into the experiences of David, Hezekiah, and Daniel.

1. David

Read Psalm 17:1–8. Write out verse 8.

_____

_____

_____

David asks God to hear his prayer and seems to give Him reasons for listening. Then he asks Him to give special favor when He does listen. He wants God to lean out of heaven for him. David wants God's *ear* and *eye*, His undivided attention. He wants His most tender affection and jealous care.[1] I don't think David is trying to strong-arm God into giving him what he wants because he is obedient. He is simply saying, "I love you with my life, Lord. You've got MY ear and MY eye. Here is how I'm trying to show it."

David understood the direct relationship between how he chose to live his life, loving God, and how God responded to his prayers. What boldness to request God's *ear*! What confidence in the intimacy of the relationship to ask to be **the apple of His eye**—and this from someone already familiar with sin and his propensity for it (Psalm 19:12-13). Clearly, perfection is not required for the attentiveness of God, because God gives it freely and exceeded David's expectations (2 Samuel 22 is a perfect example):

> David sang to the LORD the words of this song
> when the LORD delivered him from the hand of
> all his enemies and from the hand of Saul.
>
> 2 Samuel 22:1

Do you want God's ear? Do you want to live as if He is leaning over heaven's edge to be gracious to you? If these are your ambitions, tell Him. Describe where you are today and where you want to go with Him.

_____

_____

_____

_____

2. King Hezekiah

We were introduced to King Hezekiah in week 5. The Bible gives two noteworthy facts we have not yet investigated about this king:

> He did what was right in the eyes of the LORD, just as his father
> David had done. . . . Hezekiah trusted in the LORD. . . . He held
> fast to the LORD and did not cease to follow him; he kept the
> commands the LORD had given Moses.
>
> 2 Kings 18:3, 5-6

There were two instances in Hezekiah's life that speak to the attentiveness of God to his prayers. We studied the first, involving the Assyrians, previously. Hezekiah took his troubles directly to God, laid them on the table, asked for help, and trusted God to act on his behalf. Recall with me God's response in Isaiah 37:21.

_____

_____

At some point, Hezekiah developed a serious illness. Isaiah the prophet came as God's messenger to tell him he was going to die (Isaiah 38:1). True to his character, Hezekiah's first response was to turn his face to the Lord (vv. 2–3). Notice how quickly he received a response from the Lord:

> Before Isaiah had left the middle court, the word of the LORD
> came to him: . . . "I have heard your prayer and seen your tears;
> I will heal you."
>
> 2 Kings 20:4–5

Don't miss the connection. Hezekiah's immediate response was turning to God because that is where he placed his security. Before the prophet had exited the building, God, in turn, *heard* and *saw*.

*The eyes of the L*ORD *are on the righteous, and his ears are*
attentive to their cry.

Psalm 34:15

3. Daniel

Daniel (also introduced in week 5) was a captive from Jerusalem, taken into the service of King Nebuchadnezzar of Babylon. He took seriously the call to love the Lord completely. Several events illustrate his commitment and complete reliance on God. When he was instructed to eat food unlawful for God's people, instead of simply giving in to the demands before him, Daniel *"resolved not to defile himself with the royal food and wine, and he asked the chief official for permission not to defile himself this way"* (Daniel 1:8).

The rest of his life, time and time again, Daniel made choices to love his God in spite of dire and deadly consequences. In fact, even his enemies reported they *"could find no corruption in him, because he was trustworthy and neither corrupt nor negligent"* (Daniel 6:4).

Daniel 9 records a time when Daniel prayed to the Lord and then gives us God's response. Read Daniel 9:2–23 and write how this exchange played out in Scripture.

_____

_____

_____

Have you ever experienced the immediacy of God meeting your specific need or answering a specific question? Today, do you need Him to lean into you to listen and respond? Remember, *He rises for you.* Ask.

_____

_____

_____

I absolutely love getting an immediate response from God. However, the benefit of living life, loving God with everything we are, is not receiving the desired instantaneous response but the *attention* given to the one making the request. As you and I have experienced, sometimes God does not act immediately. Sometimes His actions are not what we have requested. But whatever His response, those who seek to love Him completely have His **ear** and His **eye**.

Lord, today may we grasp your relentless pursuit of us when we seek to love you with everything we are. You obligate yourself to us. I know you are listening because 2 Chronicles 16:9 tells us that "the eyes of the Lord range throughout the earth to strengthen those whose hearts are fully committed to Him." You are looking for us! We don't have to try to pull you away from anything in order to share your attention. We simply have it. Thank you for listening. Thank you for seeing.

DAY 2

HE SHARES HIS SECRETS

Praise be to the name of God for ever and ever; wisdom and
power are his. . . . He gives wisdom to the wise and knowledge

to the discerning. He reveals deep and hidden things.

Daniel 2:20–22

Birthdays at the Strange house share a common tradition, the Birthday Trail. I'm not sure when the tradition began, but every year, late the night before each birthday, I string a trail of birthday bows, streamers, and construction-paper cards from the birthday child's bedroom, down the hall, down the stairs, around the corner, through the living room, and into the kitchen, where it leads to the pinnacle of birthday anticipation, the presents.

Like our Birthday Trail, God leads us to know Him more intimately, step by step through His Word. Anne Graham Lotz writes:

"Anyone can be blessed by just reading this truly magnificent piece of literature that spans the years of human history. But there is a unique blessing that is reserved for those who prayerfully, earnestly, and humbly approach it by faith as the truth, seeking to go past the surface reading into the deeper meaning."[2]

THE DEEPER MEANINGS REVEALED

Samuel is a prime example of someone who received this unique blessing. In a time when a word from the Lord was rare (1 Samuel 3:1), God chose to speak to a little boy ministering before him. One night, God spoke to Samuel in an audible voice about the ensuing judgment on Eli, the priest, and his unfaithful sons (vv. 4–14). But after this instance, what do we learn (v. 19)?

_____

_____

Samuel dedicated himself to giving God his ear and his eyes. And in response to his loving actions:

The LORD continued to appear at Shiloh, and there He revealed Himself to Samuel through his word.

1 Samuel 3:21

Just as is His practice today, God chose to reveal himself through His Word. What does this say to you about the power of Scripture in one who longs for and waits expectantly for her God?

_____

_____

_____

When I first began getting up early in the morning to spend time alone with God, I never imagined He might enjoy being with me. It was something I did out of obedience. One year on my birthday, I was awakened about 4:30 a.m., and I complained, "Lord, are you kidding me! Can't I sleep a little longer on my birthday?" I felt an answer come immediately from the Lord: "But Cheri, I *know* it's your birthday, and I just couldn't wait to wake you up!" That was not the response I was expecting. I began to think, *Maybe He really does delight in me. Maybe He is excited to celebrate my birthday with just me?* Of course, I got up.

"*If you seek him, you will be found by him*" (2 Chronicles 15:2). He is not checking you off a list of people to see. You are not His drudgery; you too are His delight. He totally digs you and absolutely cannot wait to be with you. What transformation my mornings have taken since realizing His love of being with me.

Just as we are reminded in the opening verse of this lesson (Isaiah 30:18), the God of the universe, who spoke everything into existence, also rises to spend time with *you* through His Word.

What does Jeremiah 29:13 record?

_____

_____

How does Jeremiah 29:13 compare with Matthew 6:33?

_____

_____

_____

SECRETS ARE OURS FOR THE TAKING

My largest mastiff (at 120 pounds and eye level with the stove top), Boston, is incredibly disciplined. Never has he attempted to get food off the counter or even out of a shopping bag left on the floor. He doesn't beg or expect table scraps. But Boston has a sweet tooth, and he's smart. He has learned that I typically snack on dry cereal while I write and that I occasionally drop a few pieces in the course of the day. He pushes his large frame through my office doors every couple of hours, licks my surroundings and helps himself to what I have dropped. If I have not dropped any cereal, he looks at me longingly and waits. (He knows I can't resist pulling more out of the bag, just to drop a few pieces for him). Coming to see me on a regular basis has become a benefit for Boston. He knows he will get his favorite combination from me: something sweet to eat and a big hug. So he keeps coming back and asking.

What does Jeremiah 33:2–3 tell us God promises to those who keep coming back and asking?

_____

_____

The Hebrew word for *unsearchable* in Jeremiah 33:3 refers to something that is made inaccessible by fortifying it or enclosing it and is used in other parts of Scripture to describe heavily fortified cities.[3] The psalmist expresses this same benefit from the Lord in Psalm 119:97–100:

> *Oh, how I love your law! I meditate on it all day long. Your commands are always with me and make me wiser than my enemies. I have more insight than all my teachers, for I meditate on your statues. I have more understanding than the elders, for I obey your precepts.*

The psalmist testifies that he understands more because he meditates on Scripture. He spends time praying, pondering, and asking God for understanding, as well as obeying what Scripture teaches. This is exactly why some Christians experience more aha moments than others. Paul explains how it works in 1 Corinthians 2:6–14. What is the key according to Paul?

_____

_____

It's not that God is holding out on regular folk and making himself known to only a few. The unsearchable things of God are available to those who seek Him. The more we pursue Him, the greater opportunity the Spirit has to reveal spiritual truths to us. Such wisdom and knowledge remain inaccessible to those who are lukewarm in their relationship to Christ or content with just going through religious motions. Paul describes these people as *"having a form of godliness but denying its power"* (2 Timothy 3:5). It is through the power of the Holy Spirit that we experience the benefits given to those who love God by pursuing Him in His Word. Don't miss it!

How do these verses encourage you to seek Him in His Word through the Holy Spirit?

> *My goal is that they may be encouraged in heart and united in love, so that they may have the full riches of complete understanding, in order that they may know the mystery of God, namely, Christ.*

Colossians 2:2

> *In Him all the treasures of [divine] wisdom (comprehensive insight into the ways and purposes of God) and [all the riches of spiritual] knowledge and enlightenment are stored up and lie hidden (v. 3, AMP).*

_____

_____

_____

_____

While writing this study, I had an unusual dream of being in a historic mansion visiting with an old man. I was sitting with him and talking over what looked like a scrapbook, asking him questions, and listening attentively to his answers and stories. It was just he and I, and he was delightful. In a few moments, the older gentleman wanted to show me something in the attic. When he opened the attic door and took me up, everywhere I looked were breathtaking and truly exquisite treasures. It was incredible. I wanted to stay, but someone came to the door below, and we had to stop for the moment.

The next morning I thought how much my dream felt like a dynamic relationship with God. There is so much more to see, to know, and experience, just as there were more treasures to explore in that attic. If my dream was even a foggy analogy of what it's like to look for Him, to experience more of Him, and delight in what He wants to show me, then at a minimum *I want to know what is in that attic!* I want to open the chests, look at the love letters, read the inscriptions on the trophies, and uncover what is covered until there is nothing left to explore.

I wonder if this is what God means when He says:

> *I am the Lord your God, who brought you up out of Egypt. Open wide your mouth and I will fill it!*

Psalm 81:10

Do you want the Spirit to have freedom to uncover hidden treasures about God for you?

Do the time.

Do you want to experience more aha moments in your daily walk?

Sit down with your Bible as if He were with you, showing you His scrapbook. Let His Word speak to you as you ponder what it says. ***Then get ready to open wide.***

DAY 3

YOU KNOW WHAT TO DO AND PEACE PERMEATES

It's in Christ that we find out who we are and what we are living for. Long before we first heard of Christ, and got our hopes up, he had his eye on us, had designs on us for glorious living, part of the overall purpose he is working out in everything and everyone (Ephesians 1:11–12 MSG).

THE BENEFIT OF PURPOSE

Do you know what you are living for? Do you know what you are to do with your life? My children talk freely about their aspirations. I live with girls who dream of being teachers, dancers, doctors, artists, and one policeman/singer combo—unless she wants to preach. (She hasn't decided.) I live with boys who dream of becoming superheroes like firefighters and pilots. Funny, I have no children hoping to become aimless. No one speaks of aspiring to be average. No one is looking to waste a chance to make a difference. You and I are no different. We dream of purpose. Fortunately, we find ours in Christ.

My friend Erin has a little boy with layers of medical issues. Several different specialists have identified some problems with him, but no one has looked at this child with one overarching plan of action, until now. Erin just finished meeting with a new doctor who listened to all she said, looked at all the reports, and gave her a strategy for finding how to help her baby. He told her what they would try first. If that did not work, he explained what would follow those steps, and so on. For the first time, this precious young mom has comfort because she found someone with a plan.

How can the following verses comfort us in knowing someone has a plan?

Isaiah 46:10–11

_____

_____

Jeremiah 29:11

_____

_____

God knows the plans, but how do we come to know His plans for us? We spent time reflecting on the first part of Romans 12:2 in week 5. What can this verse teach us about recognizing His purpose for our life?

> *Do not be conformed to this world (this age), [fashioned after and adapted to its external, superficial customs], but be transformed (changed) by the [entire] renewal of your mind [by its new ideals and its new attitude], so that you may prove [for yourselves] what is the good and acceptable and perfect will of*

God, even the thing which is good and acceptable and perfect
[in His sight for you] (AMP).

_____

_____

_____

Not only does God hold the overall plan for all creation throughout eternity, He has plans for individuals, like you and me and my friend Erin, *"good and acceptable and perfect"* plans. Christ has no plans of mediocrity for you. No. Not for you.

It is in Christ we find life and our purpose. When we desire the details of His purpose for our lives, the key is to *keep seeking*. My dog, Boston, has been in my office about five times this afternoon looking for what satisfies his sweet tooth. We need to practice the same diligence and commitment until we know *"his good, pleasing and perfect will"* (NIV) for our lives.

How have the specific details about God's purpose for your life been revealed to you?

_____

_____

_____

What questions still remain?

_____

_____

_____

Keep seeking. You are not the one outlier or the forgotten daughter, regardless of age or ability. You have purpose. *What He has planned, that He will bring about . . . using you.*

THE BENEFIT OF PEACE

The LORD gives strength to his people;
the LORD blesses his people with peace.

Psalm 29:11

I cannot explain it. There is a peace that is derived from God alone. It is something He freely gives the believer in a supernatural way that cannot be explained. Often, people who have faced danger, disaster, loss, injustice—situations that beg the question why—articulate peace coming upon them in a remarkable fashion. Such peace is even physically apparent. Certainly, this is a precious gift from the Lord that affects not only the child of God but the world around her. Psalm 119:165 says:

Great peace have those who love your law, and nothing can
make them stumble.

What about you? Have you experienced the undeniable and unexplainable peace that comes from God? Describe your experience.

_____

_____

_____

_____

There is another kind of peace available to those who seek hard after God, but this kind requires our cooperation. Read these three verses in Isaiah. What do we need to do to take hold of the peace we have been given?

Isaiah 26:3

_____

_____

Isaiah 26:12

_____

_____

Isaiah 48:18

_____

_____

Life is booming with peace stealers. I think this is why Jesus said to His disciples:

> *"Peace I leave with you; my peace I give you. I do not give to you as the world gives. Do not let your hearts be troubled and do not be afraid."*
>
> John 14:27

Jesus commanded His disciples not to let their hearts be troubled. This word is for us as well. Remember, fear is juxtaposed with peace. Fear is a hindrance to wholehearted pursuit because we begin to place doubts between ourselves and the Lord. But peace begins to permeate and fragrance our lives as we resist the temptation to fear what comes our way, to resist fretting over the difficulties in our lives and pondering all that may or may not happen, to refrain from replaying that terrible situation again and again, sucking the joy out of life. Otherwise, giving in to these temptations sends us spiraling into internal misery—ugh! I can move from peaceful into the spiral of misery in less than five minutes.

What do you do when you want to choose the benefit of peace but the spiral of misery calls out to you? In all my academic wisdom and experiential knowledge, may I suggest one thing? ***STOP IT!*** Stop that downward spin in your thinking.

A few years ago, I went through a very difficult time, emotionally and spiritually. My thoughts were consumed with the situations in my life that worked to keep me perpetually in the spiral of misery. But I began to give those thoughts over to the Lord and embrace the peace of His Word to me. My sister, Kim, who was familiar with all I went through, asked me later how I got through it. I told her, "I just had to stop it." I had to continue to choose peace over turmoil and misery until I could get through a day, then a week, then a month before I found myself thinking any of those thoughts again. Then I replaced those thoughts with healing measures of the Word of God.

This is the same advice offered by Paul in Colossians 3:15. Record his suggestion:

_____

_____

_____

The Greek word for *rule* literally means "to function like an umpire" in all human relationships.[4] "It is to act with decisive force in the conflict of impulses or feelings that may arise in a Christian life."[5] So many times I have failed. But what I am learning to do to get free from the internal cycle of misery—and experience life as Christ intends—is to let the peace of Christ rule in my mind and heart rather than allow my thoughts and fears to keep me in turmoil.

Are you choosing to take hold of the peace of Christ and let it rule over the chaos in your life? Is there a past or present situation keeping you knotted and filled with anxiety? Are there certain people in your life who have this effect on you? It's time to act decisively on your impulses and feelings. What would the peace of Christ approve of in your situation? I needed to stop one trail of thought and replace it. What should you do?

_____

_____

_____

_____

_____

> *Now may the Lord of peace himself give you peace at all times*
> *and in every way. The Lord be with all of you.*
>
> 2 Thessalonians 3:16

DAY 4

YOUR CERTAINTY SWELLS AND FRUIT IS PLENTIFUL

Job is someone who displayed certainty in the midst of calamity, for sure. Here we find a man completely faultless in bringing his current circumstances upon himself. He has lost everything, including his livelihood, his possessions, ALL his children, and the respect of his wife. His skin is literally peeling away. His friends, rather than comfort him in a time of desperate need, accuse him of living in sin; they believe these terrible tragedies are consequences of his sin. Job is completely alone in his suffering and loss. There is absolutely nothing in his life that gives any glimmer of hope, much less certainty, but he has it.

SWELLING CERTAINTY

Read Job 19:25–27 and underline three things Job knew:

> *I know that my redeemer lives, and that in the end he will stand*
> *upon the earth. And after my skin has been destroyed, yet in my*
> *flesh I will see God; I myself will see him with my own eyes—*
> *I, and not another. How my heart yearns within me!*

Can you feel the emotion of Job? Why do you think these three elements were so important to him?

_____

_____

_____

What about you? Has there been a time when your circumstances left you devastated? When you, like Job, felt completely alone?

_____

_____

_____

Job found certainty in the midst of calamity because he spent the days prior loving God with his life. The book opens by telling us, *"This man was blameless and upright; he feared God and shunned evil."* Job was living the Greatest Commandment to the extent that he had God's *ear* and His *eyes*. God boasted of Job's love before Satan by saying, *"Have you considered my servant Job? There is no one on earth like him; he is blameless and upright, a man who fears God and shuns evil"* (Job 1:8). Job found certainty in the middle of hopelessness because he *knew* his God.

Read 2 Timothy 1:8–12. Here Paul explains his own suffering for loving God with his life. According to verse 12, what does Paul know?

_____

_____

_____

What does it mean to you that these two men who loved God completely found certainty because of what they knew?

_____

_____

We can also find certainty in God's commitment to us. Read Hebrews 13:5 (AMP) and circle the phrases that communicate His unbreakable bond to you:

> Let your character or moral disposition be free from love of
> money [including greed, avarice, lust, and craving for earthly
> possessions] and be satisfied with your present [circumstances
> and with what you have]; for He [God] Himself has said,
> I will not in any way fail you nor give you up nor leave you
> without support. [I will] not, [I will] not, [I will] not in any
> degree leave you helpless nor forsake nor let [you] down
> (relax My hold on you)! [Assuredly not!]

I just wonder if you need to know right now that your God will not leave you without support, even if others do. He will not leave you helpless, even though it might be how you feel. He will not give you up, even if another has. He won't. He is holding you. He will not, will not, will not let go.

Underline the words below in Hebrews 13:6 (AMP) that describe the confidence we gain because of the surety of God's love for us:

> So we take comfort and are encouraged and confidently and
> boldly say, The Lord is my Helper; I will not be seized with
> alarm [I will not fear or dread or be terrified].
> What can man do to me?

Unmistakably, a true benefit of living to love God with our lives is certainty. How can this unbreakable commitment to you and the encouragement it brings impact your life today?

_____

_____

_____

_____

PLENTIFUL FRUIT

Christ came so that we would have a life that overflows (John 10:10). He wants us to know Him, find our very existence in Him, and reap the benefits of this relationship. But this is not simply for our good. In reality, our life is really not about us. It's about *them*. Jesus is clear about this in John 15:16. Write the verse:

_____

_____

_____

_____

Paul tells us in Romans 7:4 that bearing fruit is the point of Christianity:

> So, my brothers and sisters, you also died to the law through
> the body of Christ, that you might belong to another,
> to him who was raised from the dead,
> in order that we might bear fruit for God.

One of the benefits of seeking to love God with all our hearts, souls, minds, and strength is that we stop thinking so much about ourselves and turn our focus to *them.*

In Christ, you and I have been given what is necessary for becoming *them*-focused and living fruitful lives. Do you remember 2 Peter 1:3, which tells us we have been given "*everything we need for a godly life*"? If the point of Christianity is to go and bear fruit, having "*everything we need*" should equip us for anything we might encounter.

Bearing fruit is directly related to our commitment to the Greatest Commandment and receiving the benefit of full living. We see this close connection in 2 Peter 1:3–8. According to Peter, what qualities does bearing fruit require?

_____

_____

_____

How would you explain our ability to control whether we possess these qualities *"in increasing measure"* as described by Peter?

_____

_____

_____

Peter's message is encouraging because he connects our call to bear fruit, our equipping to bear fruit, and the benefit of bearing fruit to living effective and productive lives. I want my life to be effective and productive. I want what Charles Spurgeon describes that comes only to those whose hearts are completely motivated toward loving God with all:

> *"Let your heart be perfumed with affection for men's souls. So live that men may take knowledge of you that you have been with Jesus, and have learned of Him."*[6]

Tomorrow, after I finish writing the final entry in this study, I'm spending the afternoon tending my roses. Individual rose bushes line our long driveway and are in desperate need of attention. My husband hates these roses and wants to pull them out. But I have promised to spend time, energy, and even money on them this year to see if I can improve their current scraggly state. I envision full bushes exploding with color—red, yellow, coral, white, and pink—greeting me as I pull up to my house. But in order for this vision to ever become a reality, I must give each bush a severe pruning.

God needs to do the same thing with you and me. In order for our lives to reflect His vibrancy and color, He will need to do some pruning. If you and I are going to reach our full potential in fruit bearing, we need to allow Him to prune, even if it be severely, anything that needs to go. In John 15:1–2 Jesus says:

> I am the true vine, and my Father is the gardener. He cuts off
> every branch in me that bears no fruit, while every branch that
> does bear fruit he prunes so that it will be even more fruitful.

Let's agree to allow Him to do some pruning. Yes, it might smart a little—but you and I will reap the benefits all the more. I thank God we have been given everything we need to live fruitful lives. What a blessing! What a privilege to live lives that reach beyond ourselves. Right now, I pray that God would move so greatly in your heart that you would begin (or continue) to bear fruit in increasing measure. How would He have you respond today?

_____

_____

_____

_____

> And God is able to bless you abundantly,
> so that in all things at all times, having all that you need,
> you will abound in every good work.
>
> 2 Corinthians 9:8

Day 5

You Triumph over Obstacles

> *Now to Him Who, by (in consequence of) the [action of His]*
> *power that is at work within us, is able to [carry out His*
> *purpose and] do superabundantly, far over and above all that*
> *we [dare] ask or think [infinitely beyond our highest prayers,*
> *desires, thoughts, hopes, or dreams]—To Him be glory in the*
> *church and in Christ Jesus throughout all generations*
> *forever and ever. Amen (so be it).*
>
> Ephesians 3:20–21 AMP

Think about what this passage means. No matter your circumstances, your family heritage, or your history of stupid mistakes, your life story can overflow with fulfilled promises. You can triumph over your obstacles to accomplish all He has called you to do. Remember, He is not demanding perfection but a life that yearns for Him as one who makes Him wait no longer. When you live to love Him wholly and completely, *be ready*. He intends to do far over and above all we dare ask or think possible—infinitely beyond our highest prayers, our deepest thoughts, our hopeless hopes, and our most far-fetched dreams, even when we least expect it.

Consider Catherine Booth, a painfully shy and reserved woman too terrified to speak to a small group of children—who found her voice leading others to care for the poor and destitute.[7] In a matter of years, through her bold speech about the biblical responsibility to care for the needy, this once-quiet wallflower rallied enough support for living out the gospel that The Salvation Army was born. Her vision and leadership touches millions long after her death, far exceeding anything she could have dared ask or imagine.

This is the kind of experience God designs for His people, the kind that gives Him the opportunity to do superabundantly far and above anything we could possibly fathom. That, my friend, is His style.

In the Old Testament, God demonstrates this relationship through His desire for those who trust in Him to have victory over enemies. Time and time again, Scripture bears witness of God's power at work, enabling His people to accomplish impossible feats against nauseating odds.

According to the following verses, how does Scripture testify to God's desire for victory and His tendency to do the astounding through His people?

Deuteronomy 20:4

> *For the LORD your God is the one who goes with you to fight for*
> *you against your enemies to give you victory.*

_____

_____

Judges 3:12–30

_____

_____

Judges 3:31

_____

_____

Judges 7:1–7

_____

_____

1 Samuel 1:1–19; 2:1–5

_____

_____

1 Chronicles 11:11–14

_____

_____

Psalm 44:4–7

> *You are my King and my God, who decrees victories for Jacob.*
> *Through you we push back our enemies; through your name we*
> *trample our foes. I put no trust in my bow, my sword does not*
> *bring me victory; but you give us victory over our enemies,*
> *you put our adversaries to shame.*

_____

_____

Does this quest for victory and vanquishing foes continue into the New Testament and the coming of Christ? Yes, but it takes on a spiritual dimension. Where we tend to read about victories in the Old Testament, we find overcoming prevalent in the New Testament. Where God is responsible for making each victory possible in the Old Testament, Jesus is the centerpiece in the New.

 WORD STUDY

The English word, overcome, comes from the Greek word, nikē, meaning victory. In short, overcome means "to overpower; to conquer; and to triumph,"[8] and implies that there is a battle involved.[9]

The following verses help us become familiar with this concept in the New Testament. How do these verses speak to God's tendency toward displaying His power and His desire for Christ-exalting triumph?

John 16:33

_____

_____

Romans 8:35–37

_____

_____

Romans 12:21

_____

_____

1 John 5:4–5

> *For everyone born of God overcomes the world. This is the victory that has overcome the world, even our faith.*
> *Who is it that overcomes the world? Only the one who believes that Jesus is the Son of God.*

_____

_____

Revelation 21:6–7

_____

_____

We know God's plans for us includes overcoming our obstacles. We know it's worth it. And we understand this capability is ours, given by the one who loves us more than we can comprehend. **But just how do we do it?**

Hebrews 12:1–3 (MSG) shows us the way.

> *Do you see what this means—all these pioneers who blazed the way, all these veterans cheering us on? It means we'd better get on with it. Strip down, start running—and never quit! No extra spiritual fat, no parasitic sins. Keep your eyes on Jesus, who both began and finished this race we're in. Study how he did it. Because he never lost sight of where he was headed—that exhilarating finish in and with God—he could put up with anything along the way: Cross, shame, whatever. And now he's there, in the place of honor, right alongside God. When you find yourselves flagging in your faith, go over that story again, item by item, that long litany of hostility he plowed through. That will shoot adrenaline into your souls!*

HOW DO WE TRIUMPH OVER OBSTACLES?

How exactly do you and I get on with the business of overcoming every obstacle? Because in all reality, we will find ourselves "flagging in our faith" from time to time. Thanks be to God for not leaving us to fend for ourselves. We can take our queues from those who have walked before us and shown us the way.

RECOGNIZE THE TASK

When Taylor (my oldest daughter) began as a long-distance runner in school, every day as we drove home from practice, she confessed that she had not done her best. Instead, she stayed in the back with her friend. On race day, I explained the sobering truth: "Taylor, it's a race. It's not a moving social club. Your coach expects you to give it all you've got. Get in there and do your best, even if it means leaving your friend in the dust!"

The same is true for us. The call on our lives is not to a stroll or a saunter, but a race.[10] How does Colossians 4:5 relate to this call?

_____

_____

FIND ENCOURAGEMENT IN THE CLOUD

> *Therefore, since we are surrounded*
> *by such a great cloud of witnesses, . . .*
>
> Hebrews 12:1

When I ran the Oklahoma City Memorial Marathon, people lined up along the entire course cheering me and my ten thousand companions toward the finish line. People I did not know urged me to keep going. They thanked me for running, for the reason for running this race was to remember the tragic loss of lives in the Oklahoma City bombing. Total strangers insisted I could make it. My physical and mental struggle was obvious in those difficult miles, but onlookers pushed me farther down the path with their uplifting reminders of why I was running. I crossed that finish line accompanied by great applause from strangers gathered for a common purpose and goal. That is the picture the writer of Hebrews is painting for us.

We are encouraged to think about those who have come before us. When we remember their stories, their trials, their sufferings, and their faith in finishing the race marked out for them, our courage is aroused. I suspect this is why the chapter begins with *"Therefore,"* connecting the great cloud of witnesses with the testimonies in Hebrews 11 of those who finished strong. From this encouragement, we can take one more step. And then another and another.

My marathon experience caused me to recognize my need for support along this long-distance spiritual race we are running. Are you in need of the same? Imagine me standing on the sidelines holding a poster with your name on it, screaming and clapping wildly for you. What would you need me to say that would cheer you farther down the path toward the finish line?

_____

_____

_____

Consider it done. But if that is insufficient, I have prayed God would send you an encouraging word.

THROW OFF EVERYTHING THAT HINDERS

> *Let us lay aside every weight, . . .*
>
> Hebrews 12:1, KJV

The word *weight* includes anything that would put you at a disadvantage in running.[11] We tend to think of these as negative or sinful things that hold us back, but they could well be innocent things that keep us from running our best and impede progress.[12] For me, HGTV hinders my progress. Scrapbooking and Pinterest hinder my progress, because my race requires a great deal of focused attention. Are they sinful endeavors? No, but they must be abandoned for this season.

Think about your own race. What comes to mind when you think about things in your life that might weigh you down or hinder you from running your race?

_____

_____

_____

_____

DEAL WITH SIN

And the sin that so easily entangles.

Hebrews 12:2

The sin that easily entangles is personal. It's the one you chide yourself over most often. It's the temptation that works every time, or at least consistently. You know the one. You promised yourself you **WOULD NOT** yield to it. Then suddenly you find yourself in the middle of it. None of us are immune. What sin trips you up? Where is your weak spot that keeps you from running the race?

_____

_____

_____

One commentator wrote, "If we do not renounce sin, we give up the race."[13] Are you willing to renounce it right here; right now?

_____

_____

_____

RUN OUR COURSE

And let us run with perseverance the race marked out for us, . . .

Hebrews 12:2

In week 6, I mentioned my sweet friend Lisa and her need for greater strength. Her condition has worsened. If my friend's body continues to systematically shut down on her at midlife and she increasingly loses mobility (with children still under her wing, a family business, and a husband), is she living life to the full as Christ intends? Is she experiencing the kind of life God dreams for her? Can God move superabundantly in her life, with a broken-down body, and likely some days a broken-down heart to match—far more than she can ask or imagine?

According to the Word of God, yes. We are to run the race marked out for *us*. Lisa's course is marked, just like an official race is mapped out, perfectly planned. *Her* performance in this race is compared against *her* course—not mine, and not yours. If she throws off what hinders *her* from loving God in the midst of difficult circumstances with everything she is, if she renounces the sin that entangles *her* and spiritually runs *her* course—the life God planned for *her*—with perseverance, then yes, she will have triumphed over her obstacles to live life to its fullest. And I have no doubt that her God will demonstrate that she is His favorite by straining over the edge of heaven to meet every need in each step of her course in ways that will absolutely astound her and all who are privileged to know her.

We should stop trying to compare our courses with those of the women next to us. What does it mean to you that God has prepared a course for *you*?

_____

_____

_____

FIXING OUR EYES ON CHRIST

In a long-distance race, there are pacers, experienced runners who run with a flag announcing how fast they will run across the entire race. Runners line up behind the pacer that matches their average speed. Each runner's job is to try to keep up with the pacer. It's sort of a catch-me-if-you-can game that keeps runners on pace, giving them a guide all the way to the finish line.

Jesus is the leader of our race, holding up the flag we are to follow. He is **the standard**. He has gone before us and finished His race victorious over every sin, every trial, every temptation, and even death itself. It is His example we are to follow in suffering. It is His life we are to model in obedience to the Father. It is He who understands loneliness and exhaustion. It is Jesus who knows the depth of our own depravity and came to rescue us anyway.

Jesus understands that you and I desperately want to be found irresistible. We want to be the ones He rises for and leans down to hear. We want the King to be delighted with how we display His splendor through our lives. He too wants this for us.

But what we **need** is a Savior. We need someone to rescue us from ourselves and all that comes to steal, kill, and destroy us. That's why He endured the cross. That's how He could scorn its shame. That is how He found joy through agony, and satisfaction through sacrifice. He knew we needed a Savior. ***That's why He loved us first***.

What else can we do but respond to this love, by learning to love Him with everything we are?

With all our hearts,

With all our minds,

With all our souls,

And with all our strength . . .

Until our race is won.

ENDNOTES

1. BibleHub.com. Cambridge Bible for Schools and Colleges, text from Biblesupport.com, Psalm 17:8. (Retrieved Nov. 3, 2014). http://biblehub.com/commentaries/cambridge/psalms/17.htm

2. Anne Graham Lotz, *My Heart's Cry*, (Nashville: W Publishing Group, 2002), 192.

3. Walter L. Baker, *Bible Knowledge Commentary, Old Testament*, "Jeremiah," John F. Walvoord & Roy B. Zuck, (Bible Explorer 4 software, WORDsearch, 2007).

4. Note on Colossians 3:15, *Zondervan NIV Study Bible* (Grand Rapids: Zondervan, 2002), 1857.

5. T. C. T. Croskery, *The Pulpit Commentary*, H. D. M. Spence, Joseph S. Exell, eds., (Grand Rapids: Wm. B. Eerdmans, 1962), 20:175.

6. Charles Spurgeon, *Morning by Morning*, (Nashville: Thomas Nelson, 2000), 69.

7. Ace Collins, *Stories Behind Women of Extraordinary Faith* (Grand Rapids: Zondervan, 2008), 19–30.

8. Goodrick & Kohlenberger, *Zondervan NIV Exhaustive Concordance.*

9. BibleHub.com HELPS Word-studies by Helps Ministries, Inc., 1987. (accessed November 6, 2014). http://biblehub.com/greek/3528.htm

10. C. Jerdan, *The Pulpit Commentary*, H. D. M. Spence, Joseph S. Exell, eds., (Grand Rapids: Wm. B. Eerdmans, 1962), 21:364.

11. Ibid.

12. W. Jones, *The Pulpit Commentary*, H. D. M. Spence, Joseph S. Exell, eds., (Grand Rapids: Wm. B. Eerdmans, 1962), 21:372.

13. Jerdan, *The Pulpit Commentary*, 364.

NOTES

Works Cited

Alcorn, Randy. *The Treasure Principle.* Sisters: Multnomah Publishers, 2001.

Allen, Ronald B. *The Expositor's Bible Commentary.* Edited by Frank E. Gaebelein. Vol. 2. 13 vols. Grand Rapids: Zondervan Publishing House, 2012.

Baker, Walter L. "Bible Knowledge Commentary Old Testament." *Bible Explorer 4 software.* CD-ROM. Edited by John F. Walvoord and Roy B. Zuck. WORDsearch Corp. n.d.

Barna, George. *Think Like Jesus.* Nashville: Integrity Publishers, 2003.

Binnie, W. *The Pulpit Commentary.* Edited by H.D. M. Spence and Joseph A. Exell. Vol. 2. 22 vols. Grand Rapids: Wm. B. Eerdmans Publishing Company, 1958.

Blackaby, Richard. *Unlimiting God.* Colorado Springs: Multnomah Books, 2008.

Caffin, B.C. *The Pulpit Commentary.* Edited by H.D. M. Spence and Joseph S. Exell. Vol. 20. 22 vols. Grand Rapids: Wm. B. Eerdmans Publishing Company, 1962.

Chapman, C. *The Pulpit Commentary.* Edited by H.D. M. Spence and Joseph S. Exell. Vol. 4. 22 vols. Grand Rapids: Wm. B. Eerdmans Publishing Company, 1962.

Chapman, Gary. *The Five Love Languages: The Secret to Love that Lasts.* Chicago: Northfield Press, 2010.

Collins, Ace. *Stories Behind Women of Extraordinary Faith.* Grand Rapids: Zondervan, 2008.

Conway, S. *The Pulpit Commentary.* Edited by H.D. M. Spence and Joseph S. Exell. Vol. 11. 22 vols. Grand Rapids: Wm. B. Eerdmans Publishing Company, 1962.

Croskery, T.C.T. *The Pulpit Commentary.* Edited by H.D. M. Spence and Joseph S. Exell. Vol. 20. 22 vols. Grand Rapids: Wm. B. Eerdmans Publishing Company, 1962.

Deane, W.J. *The Pulpit Commentary.* Edited by H.D. M. Spence and Joseph S. Exell. Vol. 14. 22 vols. Grand Rapids: Wm. B. Eerdmans Publishing Company, 1963.

Eckhart, Meister. *The Essential Writings.* New York: HarperOne, 2009.

Finlayson, R. *The Pulpit Commentary*. Edited by H.D. M. Spence and Joseph S. Exell. Vol. 17. 22 vols. Grand Rapids: Wm. B. Eerdmans Publishing Company, 1958.

Franscisco, Clyde T. *The Broadman Bible Commentary*. Edited by Clifton J. Allen. Vol. 2. 12 vols. Nashville: Broadman Press, 1970.

Given, J.J. *The Pulpit Commentary*. Edited by H.D. M. Spence and Joseph S. Exell. Vol. 16. 22 vols. Grand Rapids: Wm. B. Eerdmans Publishing Company, 1958.

Goodrick, Edward W., and John R. Kohlenberger III. *Zondervan NIV Exhaustive Condordance*. Edited by James A. Swanson. Grand Rapids: Zondervan Publishing House, 1999.

Graham, Billy. *The Holy Spirit: Activating God's Power in your Life*. Minneapolis: Grason, 1978.

Graham, Franklin, and Donna Lee Toney. *Billy Graham in Quotes*. Nashville: Thomas Nelson, 2011.

Hammond, J. *The Pulpit Commentary*. Edited by H.D. M. Spence and Jospeph S. Exell. Vol. 5. 22 vols. Grand Rapids: Wm. B. Eerdmans Publishing Company, 1962.

Hughes, Robert B., and J. Carl Laney. *Tyndale Concise Bible Commentary*. Bible Explorer 4 software: WORDsearch Corporation, 2007.

Jerdan, C. *The Pulpit Commentary*. Edited by H.D. M. Spence and Jospeh S. Exell. Vol. 21. 22 vols. Grand Rapids: Wm. B. Eerdmans Publishing Company, 1962.

John H. Traylor, Jr. *Layman's Bible Book Commentary*. Vol. 6. 24 vols. Nashville: Broadman Press, 1981.

Jones, W. *The Pulpit Commentary*. Edited by H.D. M. Spence and Joseph S. Exell. Vol. 21. 22 vols. Grand Rapids: Wm. B. Eerdmans Publishing Company, 1962.

Lloyd-Jones, D. Martyn. *The Christian Soldier: An Exposition of Ephesians 6:10-20*. Vol. 8. 8 vols. Grand Rapids: Baker Books, 2003.

Lotz, Anne Graham. *My Heart's Cry*. Nashville: W Publishing Group, 2002.

Morgan, Robert J. *Nelson's Complete Book of Stories, Illustrations, and Quotes*. Nashville: Thomas Nelson Publishers, 2000.

Orr, J. *The Pulpit Commentary*. Edited by H.D. M. Spence and Joseph S. Exell. Vol. 1. 22 vols. Grand Rapids: Wm. B. Eerdmans Publishing Company, 1958.

Piper, John. *Don't Waste Your Life*. Wheaton: Crossway Books, 2007.

—. *Think!* Wheaton: Crossway Books, 2010.

—. *When I Don't Desire God: How to Fight for Joy*. Wheaton: Crossway Books, 2004.

Rawlinson, G. *The Pulpit Commentary*. Edited by H.D. M. Spence and Joseph S. Exell. Vol. 5. 22 vols. Grand Rapids: Wm. B. Eerdmans Publishing Company, 1962.

Robertson, A.T. *Word Pictures in the New Testament Concise Edition*. Edited by James A. Swanson. Nashville: Holman Bible Publishers, 2000.

Rowland, A. *The Pulpit Commentary*. Edited by H.D. M. Spence and Joseph S. Exell. Vol. 5. 22 vols. Grand Rapids: Wm. B. Eerdmans Publishing Company, 1962.

Smith, R. Payne. *The Pulpit Commentary*. Edited by H.D. M. Spence and Joseph S. Exell. Vol. 4. 22 vols. Grand Rapids: Wm. B. Eerdmans Publishing Company, 1962.

Spurgeon, Charles H. *Morning by Morning*. Nashville: Thomas Nelson Publishers, 2000.

—. *Sermons of Rev. C.H. Spurgeon of London*. Vol. 10. 20 vols. New York: Funk & Wagnalls Company, 1900.

—. *Sermons of Rev. C.H. Spurgeon of London*. Vol. 9. 20 vols. New York: Funk & Wagnalls Company, 1900.

Thomas, B. *The Pulpit Commentary*. Edited by H.D. M. Spence and Joseph S. Exell. Vol. 17. 22 vols. Grand Rapids: Wm. B. Eerdmans Publishing Company, 1958.

Tozer, A. W. *The Pursuit of God*. Camp Hill: Christian Publications, Inc., 1982.

Turlington, Henry E. *The Broadman Commentary*. Edited by Clifton J. Allen. Vol. 8. 12 vols. Nashville: Broadman Press, 1969.